A Varied and Tender MULTIPLICITY

A Varied and Tender MULTIPLICITY

a materia medica *of plants, poems, and spells*

K Prevallet

Station Hill Press
BARRYTOWN, NY

Copyright © 2025, K Prevallet All rights reserved.

All rights reserved. Except for short passages for purposes of review, no part of this book may be reproduced in any form or by any means, electronic or mechanical, including photocopying, recording, or by any information storage and retrieval system, without permission in writing from the publisher.

Published by Station Hill Press, the publishing project of the Institute for Publishing Arts, Inc., 120 Station Hill Road, Barrytown, NY 12507, New York, a not-for-profit, tax-exempt organization [501(c)(3)].

Online catalogue: www.stationhill.org
e-mail: publishers@stationhill.org

Cover art: K Prevallet
Back page art: "Hawthorn" by Juliet Lockwood
Photo credits: Clover, © Georgy Markov | Dreamstime.com; Wormwood, © Photographieundmehr | Dreamstime.com; Lobelia, © Natalyka | Dreamstime.com
Cover and interior Design: Oxygen Design Group, Sherry Williams

Library of Congress Cataloging-in-Publication Data available
Names: Prevallet, Kristin
ISBN: 9781581772401

Manufactured in the United States

Author's statement
Athough certainly an invitation to investigate plant medicines for yourself and to cultivate pollinator pathways wherever you can, nothing in this book should be interpreted as medical advice. The histories recounted here are rooted in source texts and teachers who themselves are rooted in stories and remedies passed down through many generations of people, all over the planet; they are as multiple as the plants themselves and should be independently researched, verified, and explored in further depth. The poetic lens through which I am interacting with these plants is personal; yet, I hope the thoughts expressed here will be cast into the wider field of the vast and tender natural world of which we are all only a small part.

Land Acknowledgment
In the spirit of truth and equity, it is with gratitude and humility that we acknowledge that the Institute for Publishing Arts, Inc. and Station Hill Press reside on the sacred homelands of the Munsee and Muh heaconneok people, who are the original stewards of this land. Today, due to forced removal, the community resides in Northeast Wisconsin and is known as the Stockbridge-Munsee Community.

For Sophie Aster

To reunite in those mild fields of happy Eternity Where thou & I in undivided Essence walkd about Imbodied. thou my garden of delight & I the spirit in the garden Mutual there we dwelt in one another's joy

— William Blake, from *The Four Zoas: Night the Seventh*

we who love yet die every day from the lack

everything that falls is gravity including love, everything inert is
molecular movement including tumor, in vacuum everything is dust,
everything moving is never still, every rock is slowly wobbling as particles
within it collide, and every river moves faster than every rock.
Some particles move slowly, some fast; everything decaying as it grows,
everything shifting; everything nebulous, in motion, evolving;
waves move light and signals move neurons;
everything still even while blooming.

CONTENTS

Preamble   9
Anise   12
Slippery Elm   14
Wormwood   19
Boneset   22
Sunflower   24
Poke   27
Pomegranate   30
Plantain   32
Nettle   34
Holly   36
Aster   38
Geranium   40
Mugwort   43
Feverfew   47
Oak   50
Hawthorn   52
Holy Basil   56
Aloe   60
Arnica   62
Apple   64
Mandrake   67
Lichen   69
Cinnamon   71

Ginseng   74
Yarrow   79
Kudzu   81
Rhubarb   84
Thyme   87
Raspberry   89
Dead nettle   91
Amaryllis   93
Apricot   96
St. John's Wort   98
Rose   104
Dandelion   106
Rosemary   108
Red Clover   112
Frankincense   117
Aspen   119
Lobelia   124
Pine   127
Wild Cherry   129
Sage   132
Provenance and Citations   136
About the Author   144

PREAMBLE

This book is a gathering of poems—some which were published in literary magazines and anthologies, some which were rejected or never sent out—between 2002 and 2024. What connects them here, in this meadowing of language, is that they all contain signatures of subtle but symbiotic traces of plant medicines. I have been researching, using, and wondering about herbal and ecosomatic medicines since I was a teenager, watching helplessly as my mother lost a five-year battle with breast cancer. All the poems in this book are rooted in that early experience and the subsequent cascade of losses that followed; but they also reveal the joy, tenderness, intelligence, love, and healing that the plants, my great teachers, offered. As the poet Gerrit Lansing once said to me, "If you really want to learn something, the best academy to study in is the academy of trees." It is among the varied and tender multiplicity of the natural world's generous academy that these poems were composed.

  The *materia medica* (plant descriptions) foregrounds the meadow of trees and plants—the field of varied and tender multiplicities—which had originally appeared in the background of the poem. To honor the meadow, I replaced the original titles of each poem with the plant. In switching the background (nature) with the foreground (*materia medica*), the poem is pulled into the sonic and somatic fascia of its original transmission. As Maria Sledmere writes, meadowing is a process of recognizing poetry as "a multifarious site of entrance. The meadow as always entrance to something more like meadow" (*Midsummer Song*, 191). This is an act of revision which opens the field of the poems' composition to include more than the act of writing itself. After all, these poems are spells which conjure connections between human bodies and the earth. It is to counter language's aggressive potential to divide, aggravate, or inflict harm on both bodies and the earth that I offer them, alongside their corresponding plants, as spells to conjure circadian connections within you, the reader.

In writing the *materia medica* to accompany each poem, I intentionally avoided standard grammatical conventions to avoid objectifying the plants, or making it seem as if they are here only to "serve" humans. This syntax is guided by Robin Wall Kimmerer's invitation to use grammar in a way that enlivens — not dominates or encapsulates — the animacy of the more-than-human world. She writes, "If a maple is an *it*, we can take up the chain saw. If a maple is a *her*, we think twice." As a gesture towards animating the plants and trees who are integral to each poem's composition, aside from not referring to plants as an "it," I avoid using the verb "to use." Shifting syntax in this way is a gesture towards igniting animacy in place of definition.

The *materia medica* acknowledges the fields of language and earth which seed each poem. The sources for each plant cluster information assembled from books, teachers, my own botanical encounters, and internet searches. The breadth of all this information was overwhelming, and so I followed a prompt originally composed by the poet Kythe Heller for her students: "Write instructions to someone who wants to experience Kimmerer's *Grammar of Animacy* for themselves. Then take a walk, writing about the natural/more-than-human world and using each prompt for yourself as you experience all that surrounds you."

Here are the instructions which guided my *materia medica:*

• Breathing gratitude to those who have kept the knowledge of plants alive through the generations.

• Speaking of plants as worthy of respect and inclusion into the knowledge systems of which they are a part. Their evolving nomenclatures, mythologies, migrations, and fraught encounters with colonial violence are all part of their story. They are not passive receivers of names and properties; they are active participants and witnesses to how they have been used, misused, applied, stolen, collaborated with, and interpreted.

• Remaining open to the possibility of multiple interpretations.

• Allowing the plant to be both contemporary and timeless.

• Avoiding human-centered projections while acknowledging human-centered desires.

A NOTE OF GRATITUDE:
The "provenance" at the end of the book includes acknowledgments of the poems' publication, epigrams, and revision history–as well as their original titles. It also includes the sources I used to compose the *materia medica*. I would like to extend particular thanks to the T.S. Eliot House in Gloucester, MA, The Loretto Motherhouse in Nerinx, KY, Mariah Corrigan and Jon Herder, and Steve Patterson for providing the friendship, hospitality, and space for me to focus on this book. Thank you to Stacy Szymaszek, Marcella Durand, Elaine Prevallet, and Jade Hickey for providing perspective and insight into this manuscript in its various stages. Sherry Williams, thank you for your elegant design and infinite patience in working with me. And finally, much gratitude to George and Susan Quasha for including this book in Station Hill's expansive and visionary fold.

Anise

Pimpinella anisum

To eat a cake after dinner, to settle the stomach and expel gas, to thin mucus and expel it from the lungs, to soothe colicky babies, to burn seedpods as an aphrodisiac, to mix with wine and cure snakebites, to keep by the bedside for sweet dreams, to pay taxes. **Illicium verum** *[aniseed stars] of evergreen tree fruit, of powerful anti-viral containing the raw material of oseltamivir (currently patented as Tamiflu), of fostering peace and supporting grassroots momentum to stave off deadly flu epidemics. To exist between heaven and earth as good fortune, to constellate wisdoms of ancestors and past lives.*

Anise

If you were born on a Saturday, then the light of the sun caught your
    mother's eye.

Or the stars. If tipped towards Saturn, then you are quick to wit and
    long to love.

If the North Star was turned south, then you have spent your life
    looking for a home.

There are no trees — so you were born on a Monday.

The snow is silver — so you were born on a Wednesday.

Because of the day and the year that you were born, you are the
    luckiest dog in the pack.

Because of the exact moment you assembled yourself into flesh,
    you fluctuate between being temperamental and certain.

You're lucky in business. Unlucky in love. Then your luck shifts and
    the opposite happens.

Because love is a seed, you are a pod scattering stars to the wind.

If you don't find your soulmate in this life, don't worry. In the next life,
    you will be born on a Thursday.

How fortunate.

How extraordinary and lined with gold.

Because anise is the star under which you were born, your heart is a
    house and you carry a campfire always in your pocket.

Always protected. Always loved.

It's because you were born that everything has happened.

SLIPPERY ELM

Ulmus Rubra

From powerful elm family whose fuzzy-hairy flower buds are visible throughout winter, whose inner bark (phloem) is mucilage and contains more gelatine than any other natural thing. Holds indiginious medicinal wisdom as sticky, viscus friend to marshmallow root, soothing for dry throat and lungs. A porridge mixed with honey and cinnamon nourishes humans lost in the woods. As poultice for wounds, as bath to allay sores, as flush when passing kidney stones, as extractor of slivers and bullets, as lozenge when mashed with honey, as rub for a body being burned at the stake, as tea for ease in childbirth. Shapeshifts into bread, wheels, canoes, cribs, and harnesses for sleigh dogs. Currently under attack by the Elm Zigzag Sawfly whose meandering "zigzag" eating patterns threaten to defoliate leaves.

Slippery Elm

new wo-hu-man emerges as night falls through elm and into lake that is no longer lake but a hole in the ground where the water is — find the rocks and let them speak their gravely, muffled speech. Rock spinning as space-bound hum, nothing could say it better: your troubles are of the earth, silence is of the sky, aloneness is a story, it is the edge of this place. How far down goes the water hole but we don't want to fall that deep, can you get out of the muck? Belly down, slithering towards lake, not in body, rather, just skin that remembers the skin from which we came, through silk of bark, feeling heat rise from the *anima mundi*, soul of the earth, finally gathering the strength to stand, gooey & upright:

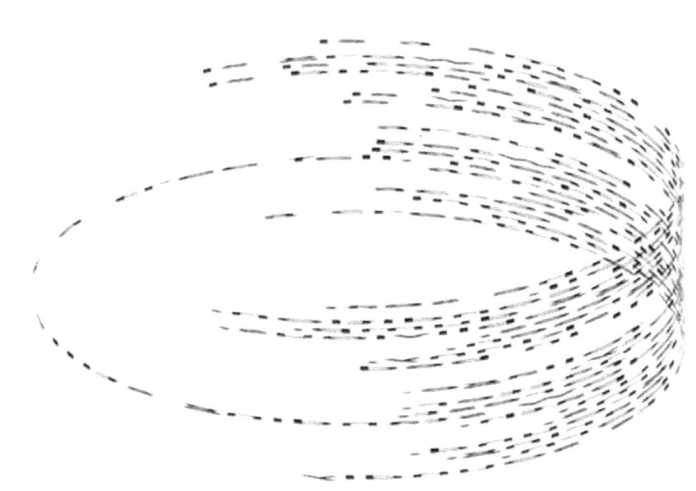

Slippery elm

is a small land the sea,
is a spill oil,
is growing a fixed condition,
is toxic a frolicking dump,
is birds' breathing oblivious,
is shade trees,
is canopy green,
is vines twist suffocating,
is daylight still bedded

the foliage between is matter
beneath forest,
if elm fell does shadow stand still?
the path of the sun,
of rhythms across the ground,
into the clearing,
where not yet born,
a creature waits

pushed out of slime interior,
chlorophyll, unlike a leaf,
cold, soon learns to fall,
such a crude awakening,
taking monstrous, sensual delight,
in continuous obliteration,
even as holding the memory of roots

Slippery elm

trees' bony elm arms claw the air,
eye campers and forest walkers,
pounce at the call of owls,
swallow small resting creatures,

soothe heavy hearts,
chip the slime from the bark,
lie in the crevice that shaped it,
walk, hesitantly at first,
until no longer embryo
a symmetry of shelters, upright,
three-tiered trunk,
worship patterns in foliage,
every leaf branches an arc,
the gods, even here,
stand firm, making bird sounds,
communicate with what has fallen

what center is trying to hold on?
out of thin air, an impossible flood,
momentarily safe on the lichen side,
then slid away,
felt slippery while drowning,
not from lungs,
but from liquid breathing

Slippery elm

beams fell,
landscape lost sound layers,
waves, just as dangerous,
born from the sludge,

grew up not rooted to the ground

made tracks,
marked forest,
entered thought,
prepared the landing

covered the canopy,
relished obliteration,
compass spinning awry

small reflections of elm leaves as
mycelium spongenetwork of memory nodes,
stepping from stone to stone with
tracks in five directions

location: many
time: simultaneous.

WORMWOOD

Artemisia absinthium

As hallucinogenic, as addictive, as effective, as extremely bitter; as volatile oil from flowerheads is called a French liquor; to be growing along fence lines and roadsides, gravel piles, overgrazed pastures and recently abandoned fields. Wants only to be used for direct purposes and for short periods of time, to invite vivid dreams, to see situations through the third eye, to expel worms and parasites.

Wormwood

My third eye opens to the brambled forest during a time in the not too distant future (given how things seem to be going) when I had to think a great deal about bears, because in this dead forest they were what is evolving. They were big and tore down my tent to get food; they climbed trees to get the fish I carefully hung for my supper, they tore open screens and ripped into plastic coolers with calm ferocity, they grew to be 20 feet tall, and were rarely seen in the winter

When I found him, he was a round thing I spotted because he was bleeding, I was snowshoeing, the snow was blanketing, I was looking for rabbits for my stew, or chinchillas for my coat; he was a red and black mound that stood out starkly, it was the heat rising from him in vapors that made me approach, drawn as I was towards suffering that wasn't my own, I could smell it, and knew something dead was lying in that place, then I realized the dead thing was breathing

Above all else, his eyes pulled me closer. They looked at me as if I were a moon—something high in the sky that he could reach out to touch, a child praying to stars, I was afraid of him, I knew that if I touched him, I would be violating the cause and the effect of loose barbed wire impaled into his tender mouth; he must have accidently bitten into it when scavenging for pine, the only trees that survived, and the rules were clear

After sapiens had destroyed so many species on the planet, including our own, it was now time to allow the ones left behind to evolve in their way, without interference. This was the end of the Anthropocene—I was not to interfere. Neither of us would survive if he were to harness his last surge of energy to tear me to pieces and leave me there, in the littered snow. Could he too know that this encounter folded the edges

of space and time? No other beings, heavenly or sentient, would know, or miss, our having existed in this moment, and so neither of us reacted with primal instincts of the past

Neither of us felt fear as I lifted his pierced and bloody mess of furness into my arms, and as he fell limply into me, I walked, one shoe in front of the other, the top level of ice not able to support the weight of him, I could only walk with great effort, and only then when I thought about how the blood pouring from his wound must surely be making him lighter

Weeks passed, no one could have known that I had built him a small dome out of dormant vines, and placed him inside of it; at the top of the dome I hung a star that I made from three icicles infused with wormwood and hardened as bark—it dangles above his wound, dripping, he is healing, and will be restored to the land of the living, and then, with his new life, he will claw me

He will blood to the dirt at the core of me, slaw me, have his way with the body that was me. I know all of this matters in the big picture, I know that in some future place a bear that should be dead is running wildly through the snow with a 3-pointed star scarred where the fur won't grow.

BONESET

Eupatorium

Is annoyed by the name "Joe Pye Weed" which is based on a made-up story of a Mohican medicine man named "Joe Pye" who supposedly "taught" settlers how to use it to treat break-bone (Dengue) fever. (In reality "Joe Pye" was not a medicine man but rather was a sachem known as Joseph Shauquethqueat who was involved in short-sighted land divestments.) To this day, to be boneset is to contain powerful medicine to relax muscles and organs, to soothe stomach, bowels, uterus and liver; to use dried (not fresh!) leaves as tea for rheumatisms and arthritis, to treat flu when symptoms are bone & muscle aches. Is also to be hung over doorways or burned to clear ghosts out of rooms and dwellings, to be a powerful conduit when contacting ancestors or spirit guides, to protect against "ghost sickness" (mysterious symptoms resulting from a person holding onto to the dead for too long after they have passed).

Boneset

Boneset carried the hair of two sisters to ground
hole into which Mountain pushed up and into their
minds swallowing them Whole and Finite
and this is why stories move so easily
from one brain into another
and why when in love we
get all feverish while falling.

The sun rose and all that heat
rose bones to skulltop
and shot straight to the sky
and this is why lunged creatures and trees
dig deep roots and stay close to water.

Selfishly, we forgot about the rest of the story.
And so here we are.

SUNFLOWER

Helianthus annuus

Ancient flower of nutrient-rich seeds ground into flour for cakes, bread, or mush, of deep purple dye for textiles and body art, of strong stalk to reinforce roof beams, of absorbing oil for skin and hair. Follower of colonial spice and land exploits and witness to the leveling of fields & forests to make way for factory farms. World traveler, now occupying millions of acres, growing as fuel (sunflower oil) for the economic engine of empires. But along fenceposts and roadsides, sunflower beams and smiles radiant hopefullness, that when alienated or caught in life's brambles, just follow young flowers as they track the sun, moving heliotropically through circadian rhythms, bringing warmth, intuitive sensing, and daylight to dark thinking.

Sunflower

A woman stands at the window. The sky is above.
The sun comes behind her. The sky is above.
She bends, picks a thread from her hem and begins pulling it tightly around her fingers. The sky is still above.
The sun bends, picks up a twig, and breaks it in three.
A bird in the tree.
The sun and the woman look at the bird in the tree.
They pause to think what they are doing.
The bird has no special significance. It is just an ordinary bird.
The sky is above.
The sun looks away from the bird and turns to face the woman.
She is looking at the garden.
He sees the garden through his peripheral vision.
It is overgrown with sunflowers.
She is overgrown with sunflowers.
She is looking beyond the sunflower and into the seed.
The seed has a message and it speaks.
The sky is still above.
Sun picks up a seed, twists it, breaks it, flings it all around.
Takes a cup and tears out its base.
Puts the seed in the cup. The sky.
Above but not parallel to the sky ran the sun with the cup of seeds.
The woman is still at the window.
The garden is still beyond the bird.
The bird is moving closer to the garden, and closer still to the sun.
Drops down, picks up a beetle.
Lying on its back, stones under its tongue.
The sky is above.

Sunflower

The beetle is still chirping. The woman is still by the window.
The sunflower and the window are the same shape.
They occupy two dimensional space.
The square and the color within the square.
The box and the person inside. She sees clearly in there.
The sky is still above, the bird still wants to swallow the beetle.
The sun throws the cup of seeds on the ground.
The woman bends down to pick it up.
To fill it with water. To drench him, and fill him up.
It was through this idea of saving the sun that the sky dropped down into the square.
There were other plants in the garden as well, and other birds in the sky.
The only ones that matter to this story are the ones in the window.
The bird. The sky.
Still above.

POKE

Phytolacca americana

With origins everywhere, "Puccoon" is Algonquin meaning a plant that contains dye; to be poke is to grow in low, rich, untended gravelly soils along roadsides, fencerows, and disturbed areas, whose plump purple berries are loved by birds and make a deep purple ink; used malevolently to sign treaties with no intention of keeping them, as well as the Declaration of Independence, as well as letters home written during the Civil War. Still to this day, purple berry fermented ink writes spells, breaks hexes, and composes binding love letters. Ingested berries do produce violent purging but the root, made into a salve, cleans the lymphatic system when applied to lumps, scars, or tumors.

Poke

Only a hunchback up to his ears he shrugged and went on his way
past the house and into the field
where one weed outgrows all the other flowers.
Kneeling down he pulls with all his might
but the roots are heavier than his coat
and so he fills his pockets as if something heavy
will lighten his load.
Startled by berry-seeking birds
that fly over his head
he sits upright and breaks in two.
Twin warblers carry him, where else?
To the garden. How else?
By the ears.

Poke

Only a hunchback up to her ears she shrugs
and goes on her way
past the garden and into the field
where one purple-berried weed out blooms all the other flowers.
Kneeling down she pulls with all her might but the dirt is heavier
and the roots are longer
than the pockets of her coat and so she cuts the lining as if
creating a hole will make her grow taller.
Startled by bees that fly into her hands
she traps what remains of their babble.
Burrowing without stinging she follows them where else?
To the sea.
How else? By flying.

POMEGRANATE

Punica granatum

Sweet and sour holding memory as first harvested fruit and probably the actual "forbidden fruit." Also the fruit Persephone tastes in the underworld, favored by many deities in many cultural traditions, symbolizing mysteries of death and rebirth. Base of muhammara sauce and anār-āvīj meat stew; contains 613 seeds (probably not precisely) to correspond with the 613 mitzvot (commandments). Fruit of passionate love, juice poured on oxen horns boosts the fertility of fields. Powerful amulet for altars when conjuring dream worlds. Resembling a mouthful of teeth situated in a jawbone to stave off tooth decay and gum disease; refastens loose teeth. Ruby red color resembles blood and nourishes heart health. Hydrating and sweet for persistent, sharpbeaked birds, bats, and ants. Even so, nomenclature carries poison: grenade is so named for the way "a shrapnel-scattering grenade imitates the seed-scattering explosion of a smashed pomegranate" (Kate Lebo).

Pomegranate

The underworld, unlit hallway littered with debris.

The bedroom, where they always return.

Small window, quilted spread, long mirror.

All spaces are enclosed.

Where they come in and out very quickly: a departure.

Where they re-enter: a transitional space.

One creates a space, but refuses to live in it.

He pulls everyone else down into hell.

Like occupying a room as an old man but inhabiting it as a child.

If one had treated another differently, would that have made a difference?

This was what existed above: robins on the edge of the pond.

It evolved: rain running down brick.

It ended: a centipede caught in a rug.

PLANTAIN

Plantago major

The Goddess Demeter tells a lovelorn maiden to wander the earth looking for her wayfaring man; wander she does, "waybroad" she is, planting herself everywhere and notoriously so. Comes to be known as "white man's footprint": "Just a low circle of leaves, pressed close to the ground with no stem to speak of, it arrived with the first settlers and followed them everywhere they went. It trotted along paths through the woods, along wagon roads and railroads, like a faithful dog so as to be near them" (Kimmerer). Still growing everywhere: asphalt cracks, sidewalks, railroad tracks, neglected parking lots, rims of discarded tires. All good travelers bring gifts and she brings medicine in her leaves which when applied directly to a wound will stop bleeding, bring relief to sores, extract poison, and soothe the bites of snakes, insects, and dogs.

Plantain

A woman at the corner of Avenue A and 12th street asked if I
would mind feeding her pigeons
while she went away on vacation.

I told her that I would feed her pigeons when they landed on my fire
escape in Brooklyn.
She said no, those pigeons in Brooklyn aren't my pigeons.
Feed them, I don't care, but you're not doing me any favors.
I fed them anyway.

The pigeons in Greenpoint, picking crumbs by the river,
Flew away and spread the message
That there was plenty of bread to go around.
They knew what the old woman didn't.
There are fences and there are clouds.
Cracks in every sidewalk are where the plantain grows.

Only when flying is there enough sky to see the big picture,
and birds see it all, upside down.

NETTLE

Urtica dioica

Tall, of leaves heavily veined and toothed, covered with bristly hairs to sting and irritate and tiny whorls of white or green flowers to soothe. Embracing contradictions, holding knowledges of fertility, courage, and protection against the spells of witches and the arrows used by elves to direct excruciating pain into joints (arthritis) — also protects horses from forest trolls and lightning. Induces visions, dreams, and knowledge medicines while walking barefoot through a patch and suffering the stings. Energizing and cooling, containing high concentrations of nutrients to purify blood and bones. Antihistamine for asthma and allergies, diuretic for passing kidney and urinary stones, anti-inflammatory for gout and rheumatism, mineralizer for sores and hemorrhoids.

Nettle

The doctor, wounded
tries with shaking hands to thread the vein
but blood pours out from the incision point.

Isn't there some law that declares the healer be alive before operating?

The disease becomes the symptom that consults the dying nurse.
They poison our blood with chemicals
get sicker and before we are restored, get worse.

And the earth—suffering, suffering.
Betting on the failure of her resources.
Veins spew oil, pour chemicals to disperse the surge,
only to poison the entire ocean.

Sludge in the blood stream.
Freezing of joints pings like a high frequency weapon.

Isn't it a strange logic to cut it open, harvest the resources even
while dying?

Bury me, a heap in the snow where frost is warm
And stinging, nettles break.

HOLLY

Ilex Opaca

Perhaps kin to broadleaf evergreens spreading in primeval forests, perhaps protecting a house against witchcraft and bolts of lightning; perhaps horses are kept in line when whipped with sharp-toothed sprigs, perhaps immunity is held against spells when berries are consulted for divination. Holding memories of festivals, decorated houses, animals and people adorned with leaves and sprigs, singing, praising, wishing for good tidings, hoping for good harvests. Holding memories of the brutality of empires, used to humiliate heretics and justify their torture. Offers strength to those suffering and crowns their gods, perhaps as if to say: I offer protection for all so plant me close to your houses and adorn your doors with my wreaths.

Holly

The blackbird sings and the baby laughs
The baby sings and the blackbird nests
Bird's babies squawk while the baby sleeps
Awakened by a plane, the blackbird perches on a smokestack
Awakened by a siren, the baby squats to pick up a spoon
The blackbird preens her feathers
The baby rushes to the bathtub to watch the water circle down the drain.
All of this in an hour
at the beginning of another year
marked by the horror of more and more wars.
The baby and the blackbird know nothing of centuries —
But it all happens this very hour.

ASTER

Asteraceae

The night sky tells of Asterae, daughter of the gods of dusk and dawn, who looks down on all the hatred, killing, corruption, and cruelty happening among humans on the earth. As she watches humans destroy themselves and pillage our planet, she cries star-shaped tears which fall to earth and land everywhere as star-shaped flowers. Flowers to drive away patriarchal cruelty and bring messages of peace, flower essences to dab on the third eye and open dream portals, flower ointments to treat dog and snake bites, flower tinctures to help pulmonary ailments, epilepsy, hemorrhages, malaria, blood circulation, and the flu. Dry flowers to hang in attics for protection against negative energies. Flowers to decorate altars and deepen spiritual connections with the divine feminine; flowers to reveal the cosmic patterns that weave all living things together, flowers as elements of exploded supernova star stuff — carbon, oxygen, silicon, and iron — to build bones, grow trees, nourish plants, form planets and all the stars in the galaxy.

Aster

i.

Caught between Wonder Woman and the Scarlet Witch
one lifts her up, the other drags her to the chasm where sadness
lives. I tell her she can choose and she says,

    but which one?

ii.
In the dream my daughter
sets off two magnificent
air balloons each looking like spaceships
adrift in the cosmos they deflate
into a pool completely alight with red & green,
oh be de-light!

iii.
Astonishing **S**creen **T**apestries **E**rase **R**age **A**blaze **E**ternity

GERANIUM

Pelargonium

First seeded in southern Africa then thrust into the colonizer's nomenclature confusion for many centuries before coming to be called Geranium, from Greek (Geranos), meaning "crane" due to seed pods resembling a stork's long bill. Known in the west as a strong scented, strong willed, sturdy flowering perennial, but holds knowledge of remedies to cure bronchitis, colic, and anemia. Good to plant on windowsills facing the direction of a perceived threat, good to plant in gardens to protect the house from evil spirits, good to make scented sugar for calming baths, good to sweeten tea when dry petals are sprinkled with sugar and rose petals.

Geranium

Weighed down with bags
casserole dishes and pies
presents for the kids
flowers for the host—
and another year is almost gone.

Snowy streets salted stairs
a football sits where it landed,
next to a knobby attempt to build a snowman.

Door opens, familiar
odor of basting and kitchen heat thick as greetings,
hugs, hello and welcome,
the old spaniel panting in the hallway
and the calico running to hide.

Candle-scented spice, dim lights, set table,
plates bright with cranberries and yams.

After dinner clanging of dishes
time for the annual game of charades,
the energy in the room is high,
it's girls against guys.

Category: movies.
heavy, afraid, depressed, death, doom!!!
small word: *a, the, an, off*!!!
Single malt and truffles,
Bartok's Rhapsody no. 2.

Geranium

The hostess on the edge of the couch
urgently forming a triangle with her hands,
then clutching them in prayer.

Church! pyramid! steeple!
Finally it's clear:
THE TEMPLE OF DOOM!

Laughter, goodbye, heavy coats.
Driving home,
the old routine,
so much to do—

Another year goes by,
Another shooting,
Another catastrophe,
Another glass of port,
Another crystal vase blooming with geraniums,
Another dog playing dead.

MUGWORT

Artemisia vulgaris

Being ancient and so when put under a pillow offers vision of anscestral lines and dreams to connect with wisdom traditions passed down within families. Being one who offers to treat diseases caused by spells and casts protections over bewitched people and animals; drives witches away and when hung in the highest rafters in the house, wards off lightning and deters the plague. When roots are made into a necklace, offers protection from dangerous animals and ghosts; when sprinkled on bonfires, offers to become a magic shield. Offers help with uncontrollable shaking and nervousness when added to a pipe, uncontrollable menstrual bleeding when eaten, uncontrollable insomnia when diluted into a tea, uncontrollable stomach disorders when made into a girdle, and uncontrollable fevers when made into beer.

Mugwort

i.

On the road of long middles tortoises
munch as they go on fields of mugwort,
entranced they move & defer grammar and sense —
they don't care about telling a story with a beginning, middle, and
end — they collect words and scatter them into a syntax all their own —
they move with wild abandon, latching every so often onto passing
landscapes, spilling seeds among roadsides, in cracks and underneath
buckles in the asphalt.

ii.

on a train looking out the window
longing for something / someone
the view is obscured by a torn scrap of paper
so libre — en in mente

iii.

the psychic reading was done in a hostile atmosphere
yet something always comes through:
burn down lightwhite candle
replace rage with
peace bravery calm protection
newemotionsenergy

Mugwort

fill you up

write

healing()begin

power(less)abuse absolute

heal(me)now

ritual quiet()time sooth:

red candle, white candle

paper and pen

metal tin and matches

set up quiet()space Say:

"circle, protect me and protect others from the energies I plan to release."

holdpaperhands redcandle

chant, shout, screamsounds

rage into red candle burns

tied up, shut up, shut down —

of playing small,

of giving power away,

of feeling violated, small and impotent —

rage into red candle burns

brighterhotterforceangerfuels

Mugwort

now firepapers burn

comfortably calm again release
circleenergy

s(l)inking back into the earth
thankyouelements watching over me
thank you higherinsight

Let the candles burn completely
out speak something soothing to your inner voice

Who, if I cried out, would hear me among the angels' hierarchies?
And if one of them pressed me suddenly against his heart?

—Rilke

FEVERFEW

Tanacetum parthenium

Exuberantly prolific, tall and wispy, small white daisy like flowers with bright yellow centers which cluster at the top, not to be confused with snakeroot which will grow close to it in an attempt to mimic and overtake. Spear-shaped leaves resemble the spear-like pain of arthritis — elf-shot arrows directing intense pain at joints. Known by other names, featherfew or wild chamomile; featherfoil, devil daisy, flirtwort, bachelor's button, maid's weed, midsummer daisy, Missouri nosebleed, prairie-dock, vetter-voo, or matricaria. Holds memories of being given to women to calm hysteria and to new mothers having trouble stepping back out into the world; perhaps remembers saving the life of a worker who fell while building the Parthenon. Parthenolides & anti-inflammatory compounds offer help to control expansion and contraction of blood vessels in the head, to prevent migraines when a few drops of the tincture are taken at the first glimmer of a headache, and then every four hours with lots of water. Chamomile and calendula befriends for gastritis and leaky gut. Growth around a dwelling keeps rats away even as bees and caterpillars congregate.

Feverfew

There's me in the backyard pulling legs off a spider
and to the question what did you do today
said nothin' just playing with dolls.

If I wrote something that seemed right but then wasn't right,
but spoke that sentence anyway, did I actually acknowledge the land or
the massacre?

There was the lie I used to tell about being a cheerleader over and over
for a long time because
it was culturally problematic and therefore made me avant-garde.

Sneaky like that, you know?
There's also the lie about feeling ok when really, I'm not.
I'm not feeling ok at all. Headache coming on.

But maybe in telling that lie, actually, I'm feeling a little better than I
thought.
If I told a lie about seeing a particular movie, and later, went to see that
same movie, well...
Time is an egg dream. Memories are a spiral.

It's a lie that trees have one circle for every year, trees do not gauge a
year by counting 365 days, what is the first day of the year to a tree?
Where does that story begin?

Such a tree perhaps talks of time in a root language that is lichen and
mycelium.

It's a lie that upon feeling a certain way I can track the moment when
suddenly, I begin to feel another — the swerve is rarely so dramatic, or so
sudden, it's just that suddenly, things have fallen apart.

Feverfew

I'm sensing in this exercise a rather radical failure—even more radical than sitting here pondering, again, for the hundredth time in oh so many years, is this day 1 really, of 15 weeks x 30 hours divided by a paycheck that condenses my brilliant mind into a quarter? That's a good lie that begins when the die is cast.

I turned to face the window, looking for some way out of the tangle.
I saw a tree, rose washed with sun not yet set; evening hued.
I saw the feverfew I planted hoping it would transform that water gobbling grass into a meadow.

Not yet time to chalk it all up to fate. To "just let it go."

I was mad. So I wrote a sentence about lying, didn't like it.
Wrote a sentence about trees, didn't like it.
Started to tell an old story about things falling apart (again).
Decided against it—just not feeling it for some reason.
Headache.

Looked around the room and wondered, is everyone having a hard time with this prompt?
Saw some people starting and stopping. Some nodding. Sleeping.
Others going with the flow.

Wrote another sentence about mycelium consciousness, didn't like it.
About consolidating a rhizome into an atom, didn't like it.

I read Rilke's "Bust of Apollo."
Change your life by magnifying your brilliance from the inside!
(Click tongue - nah)

Drop down deep into what is broken—that's where the lies are—

OAK

Quercus (Tourn.) L.

Being of 500 varieties of tree & shrub, sacred everywhere, associated with most powerful gods (Zeus, Jupiter, Dagda, Perun and Thor). Branches ward off witches, lightning-struck leaves make talismans, trunk's base forms an altar for blood offerings (pruning is not advised lest angry spirits are tangled in the roots). Bark in potions and rituals for midsummer abundance; branches twine divinations and leaves keep secrets. Acorns dropping nuts enclosed in basal cups are collected by deer, bears, hogs, humans, squirrels, raccoons, wild turkey, wood duck, woodpeckers, and jays; one's success of surviving long winters depends on generous acorn groundswells.

Oak

Because hindsight is 20/20
I'm coming back around
to try on this life for size
scaffolding layers of gook off my glasses
only to see
the real thing was just an altar
oaked to a coffin
growing 12 feet under
and not getting any younger.
What an oak – took a little seed
and flew it clear across the country
to twist a knot
in my tender heart.
Sadness eclipsed the child
loyalty tamed her dog;
both developed symptoms,
so deeply unconscious
that 10,000 lonely
hunters could not stifle nor shoot:
the bear in the barrow
the blood on the roots
the rainwater in the wheel
upon which so much depends.

HAWTHORN

Crataegus L

Threshold tree or shrub, portal to other worlds, so be careful not to fall through the thin line that separates this world from another. Farmers plow around so as not to fall through; mothers use the wood to make cradles and protect infants from being snatched by fairies. Broken hearted ones, the flowers bear the signature of the heart, so three droplets of essence helps move you through the threshold between old lover and new life. Tea from berries soothes aching hearts, strengthens heart muscles, improves oxygen uptake by the heart, improves circulation in the heart, and dilates blood vessels in fingers and toes so as to reduce strain on the heart. Branches braid and web dense leaves as home to nesting birds; small fruits delight cedar waxwings, fox sparrows, and ruffed grouse.

Hawthorn

i.

Trying again and again to make words make sense of a world that will never again feel complete,

My heart is aching and my bones are shaking and nothing I can do can completely overcome my attachment to you,

This just means that without you, I am not complete.

I want her back, I want him back, I want the spotted owl and the giant short-faced bear back,

I want Lyall's wren and the ivory-billed woodpecker, I want all extinct creatures back,

If I put language into the spell of rhythm can I conjure something into this space that has been long gone but here, now, is real?

If I put language into rhythms & slots

Can I conjure & remake a body,

Come again, come again,

You, they, and the birds gone,

Come again, come again

Hawthorn

ii.

If all along you had known it was a mountain, would you go, would you go through?

If in spite of it all you had known it was flaming, would you go, would you go in?

If in the midst you had known it was an arrow, would you have fallen, would you fall again?

If through the opening you had known it was a swallowing, would you be sailing, would you sail anon?

If over my dead body you knew ships passed not gently, would you hold tightly, would you hold on?

If to you I swing softly then to you I make out, would to you I come towards,

And would you let me go, let me go?

Hawthorn

iii.

a bird on a stone,

    a fish in a fish's bones,

a snake on a hook,

    a whale from some classic book,

an ant on the grass,

    a shimmering bass,

when you're gone,

    I'll remember all the bees

I have sunk all my vessels,

in your sea,

in your sea,

I have tried through it all

through it all

to be free

to be free

    when you're gone.

HOLY BASIL

Tulsi (Ocimum tenuiflorum)

First seeds may have landed in India as the incarnation of the Goddess Lakshmi (along with everything else); being aromatic and when whiffed, focusing divination and centering the third eye; being high in many nutrients plus antioxidants, dried for tea, tinctured for root, chopped for fresh leaves; being for digestion, overall circulation, and the fighting of bacterial infections. Holds sacred space in funeral rites, being the sprig placed on the chest of a dying person, being also among the herbs and barks gathered for the pyre. Being embalmed with the body, and revered in cooking as a symbol of love, protection, and hospitality.

Holy Basil

i.

Take back the preparation
the flour from the bread
the citrus from the fruit or the sweet,
take it away from the melon
make it rindy and hard
or the moisture from the clouds make them lighter
and transparent if the blue
were taken away from the sky
everything would be night
the particles from the light, take them away
make the objects of the earth disappear

Give back the teas the flowers
they came so unexpectedly
why not give back the baskets the cheese and all the meatloaf and the car
it could be given back to the driver
and pointed
in another direction give back the pine trees to the park
the parking lot to the birds or the air to silence
give back the field
to the players all could begin again
as new it all could be given back
the glacier to the snow
give back the knee-deep tread all of this
all these things could be given back and then be born again.

Holly Basil

ii.

The glacier is not cold
is not a person snow
who decides to return to water?
The wind is not dry is not a person winter
who decides there is no reason to fly?
The air is not liquid is not a person ocean
who decides there is no reason to breathe?
If the light were to expose itself as light
would there really be any reason to see?

iii.

If a person is to be saved by a herd of elk then a herd of elk will appear to the person and lead him to the sunward side of the mountain.

If a person is to be saved by a mountain lion then a mountain lion will appear to the person and lead him across the river.

If a person is to be saved by a bee then a bee will appear to a person and lead him through the sun.

If a person is to be saved by a person who understands the dow then a person who understands the dow will appear to the person and teach him about investments.

If a person is to be saved by a junkyard dog then a junkyard dog will appear to a person and lead him to the pot of gold.

If a person is to be saved by a pilot then a pilot will appear to a person and lead him through the rain.

If a person looking for an object is to be saved by a shopkeeper then a shopkeeper will appear to a person and lead him to a different object than the one he is looking for.

If a person is to be saved by a person driving a truck then a person driving a truck will appear to the person and push him off the road.

Holly Basil

If a person is to be saved by a person opening a window then a person opening a window will appear to the person and lead him into the house. If a person is to be saved by a person helping another person to jump-start a car then a person helping another person to jump-start a car will appear to the person and lead him through the electric charge. If a person is to be saved by a person walking with another person who is looking at a plane then a person walking with another person who is looking at a plane will appear to the person and lead him into the future. If a person is to be saved by a person hitting another person who was the person being hit, then the person hitting another person who was the person being hit will appear to the person and lead him to the cave.
If these people and then these people appear to a person then all these people are here to lead a person home.
If a person does not want to go home then he will be led to the mountain and there he will disappear.
If a person disappears on his way to the mountain then another person will arrive and will know that the mountain swallowed all that is green into the glacier.

ALOE

Aloe vera

First seeding in tropical climates, called "The Plant of Immortality" and "The Plant of the Blood" for holding great medicinal knowledges and a cooling gel for skin and organs. Rubbed on the wounds of Samurai fighters, embalmed with bodies in ancient Sumer and Egypt, planted at the foot of graves in the Middle East and North Africa, adorns doorways of those who made the pilgrimage to Mecca. Cathartic for lower bowels, elevates lowness of spirits, detoxifies jaundice and nourishes the liver; soothes irritated skin, burns, and damaged tissues; cools and moistens the pain of arthritis, fights cancers. When spread around the base of a white candle connects with lunar power and wisdom, especially during Esbat (full moon) rituals and divinations.

Aloe

The baby is sleeping next to the one who is no longer sleeping there.

All the sleeping that happens in a house, in the morning, when it is raining outside.

And green from all the rain outside.

The green makes the house darker than usual.

Rain makes the green light and dark, dark and light, luminous.

The particular light that is happening in the morning when everyone is sleeping.

It means something to the one who sleeps. To the one who is breathing.

But what of the one who isn't there?

Some are better in the morning than others.

Some make the fact of getting up easy, others make it heavy.

All of these things matter.

When sleeping, when raining.

All things dwell in the space of meaning.

Rain in the morning after a person is gone.

It seems impossible that one would not see this rain.

In July — it is dark when normally it is sunny.

It seems unlikely, or likely, that the sadness of this morning is the fact that one is not looking out the window.

To see how the layers of green upon green make the whole morning dark.

ARNICA

Arnica montana

Aster & daisy are family, plentiful, multiplying and versatile, appearing in all sorts of climates, as burst of orange or yellow in cracks and roadsides, fence lines, fields, and pollinator yards. Holding nomenclature confusion with leopard's bane, sneezewort, wolfsblume, and wolf's bane – erroneously translated as "wolfsleich" (wolf's corpse) or "wolfesgelegena" (wolf grass) leading Hildegard von Bingen to describe it as an aphrodisiacal plant "containing poisonous heat....When a man or woman burns with romantic desire, if someone touches him or her on the skin with Arnica while still green, they will burn with love for this person" (Physica). Carries knowledge of cooling skin to reduce swelling of burns, bruises, and wounds; soothes restless spirits inflicted by lovesickness or nervousness. Homeopathic remedy in small, highly diluted doses moves the flow of blood to the heart. Oil added to wax heightens meditations on the passing of time, reassures the uncertainty of the present moment, eases regrets and fears of failure.

Arnica

i.

In the woods I was born but not to a mother

A monster, a mutter, a mute woman with a gun

And gin, to the brim.

I begged sing to me, please,

These tunes I heard once long ago, in another life —

And she sang.

ii.

I've been alone for so long

Now that you're disappearing again

It's just me, keeping step with the day

Heavy in heart, heavy

Heavy in heart, heavy

But that's a heart for you

Broken open again and again

Hiding among the refuse,

Hiding in plain sight

Oh, how I make you out

With a target on your back

Saying you can never love a girl like me

Not like that, not like that

iii.

I began to hear the words of that song

And the hum a portal to heaven

Arnica dormant beneath ice and snow Imagination

- Imago - Mythos -

APPLE

Pyrus malus L.

Supernatural fruit holding many knowledges including fertility, abundance, beauty, magic, youthfulness, and prophesy — what spirits wait and watch from an apple tree? Branch tips dipped in spiced cider ask the spirit of the tree to bless the future harvest. Apple branches leading the way of walks into the uncertain, illegible future; knowledge of cycles, ancestors, roots of deep cultural memory that repeats with every generation. Holding gifts of flavonoids and high fiber, vitamins and antioxidant compounds, sweet as fruit eaten daily to regulate blood sugar, ease digestion, calm asthma attacks, and nourish brain cells. 3000 species branch from one ancient tree of life, all parts invite all creatures to nest and eat of fruit, seeds, buds, and bark: bears, rabbits, humans, raccoons, songbirds, flickers, finches, waxwings, and woodpecker.

Apple

Made that one sweet as pie
Then they broke me sweet as pie
Grace lies in a flower pot at my feet
I didn't mean to be lonely
I loved but slowly, preoccupied with the stars was I
Denver, Paris, Buffalo, Brooklyn

Denver, Paris, Buffalo, Brooklyn
Made that one sweet as pie
I loved but slowly, preoccupied with the stars was
Then they broke me, sweet as pie
I didn't mean to be lonely
Grace lies in a flower pot at my feet

Grace lies in a flower pot at my feet
Denver, Paris, Buffalo, Brooklyn
I didn't mean to be lonely
Made that one sweet as pie
Then they broke me sweet as pie
I loved but slowly, preoccupied with the stars was I

I loved but slowly, preoccupied with the stars was I
Grace lies in a flower pot at my feet
Then they broke me, sweet as pie
Denver, Paris, Buffalo, Brooklyn
Made that one sweet as pie
I didn't mean to be lonely

Apple

I didn't mean to be lonely
I loved but slowly, preoccupied with the stars was I
Made that one sweet as pie
Grace lies in a flower pot at my feet
Denver, Paris, Buffalo, Brooklyn
Then they broke me, sweet as pie

Then they broke me, sweet as pie
I loved but slowly, preoccupied with the stars was I
Didn't mean to be lonely
Grace lies in a flower pot at my feet:
Denver, Paris, Buffalo, Brooklyn

MANDRAKE

Mandragora autumnalis

Ignites wishes and imagination, crafts into amulets and charms, hangs upside down and nests under beds and pillows; aphrodisiac, poppet, shape-shifter, witch; human soul crying for safe passing, baby crying to be seen. Roots bear signatures of human form (limbs & organs); twine with mistletoe and place at the foot of oak to capture passing spirits of the dead. Meditating alongside roots which have taken the shape of your lover helps you to see clearly what you have gotten yourself into.

Mandrake

My lover's hair is cropped to the follicle, the follicle is white and slippery, pores open and close around it even while my lover is sleeping.
I am an upside down container, I cannot rid myself of this desire.
And so I will think about my lover's bones, they are chalky, substance of enamel and marrow,
Sturdy and connected, sinews and muscles wrap his skeleton in a heap of blood and tendons—
My lover's bones fall into my body, ambone, hipbone, leg bone, skull, I hold the skeletal part of my lover, I splay his bones in the forest like a crime scene, I bury them.
I imagine my lover's bones rotten with maggots and slime, but these thoughts of my lover's dead body fill me with sadness, I miss his bones, I want them back.
I am an upside down container, I cannot rid myself of this desire.
And so I will think about my lover's internal organs, beginning with his spleen.
The bacteria in his stomach, the bile in his liver.
My lover's lungs are meat not fit for desiring, they are tough and spongy.
I am an upside down container, I cannot rid myself of this desire.
And so I think about how alive he is with the constant movements of blood and acids, enzymes and neurotransmitters, his digesting, processing, waste eliminating, nutrition absorbing self.
Thinking about my lover as a movement of my mind brings me to my knees with ecstasy, but this is the ecstasy of a knife when not polluted by the poison of grasping.
I think about my lover's heart as it beats itself bloody, veins pop and rest in the cavity made spacious by his tender biology.
My lover's heart is the vastness of space and the absence of time, it is empty of itself as an organ but it is absolutely full of love.

LICHEN

Evernia prunastri

On trees where the air is clear an algae and a fungi live in symbiotic relationship, one deriving nutrients through photosynthesis and the other keeping the whole thing moist, on growing in the most barren of areas including Antarctica and the windblown seashores of Cape Cod, and in a variety of forms: crustose lichen are flat and crusty, foliose lichen have raised, tiny leaf- like nodes, fruticose lichen reach out all branchy and thready. As connection of opposites, as coming together to create something new, as collecting from the bones of the dead to cure elf sickness; as salve to coat the weapon that caused the wound in order to cure the wound. As a reminder of inevitable chance, as adornment for royal tombs, as a portal for connection with forest spirits.

Lichen

There is a backlog of kisses as the weeks go by
I love quiet herons and their ancient song
That strange, deep longing to which I rise

Into you I fold as deep we lie
Your body strong, and warm as the road is long
There is a backlog of kisses as the weeks go by

The birds know so many songs to guide them as they fly
They tell of love, fierce as the heron's wingspan and talon
That strange, deep longing to which I rise

I let you in where the waves are high
It is not to the night that we succumb
Oh, backlog of kisses as weeks go by

I say let's be always like the tides
They ebb, they flow but their rhythm stays strong
Like the strange, deep longing to which we rise

Or the lichen, from two species so different,
They make a new design
Connecting every pine to their song
There is a backlog of kisses as the weeks go by
That strange, deep longing to which we rise

CINNAMON

Cinnamomum cassia

*Gift of the gods, an aphrodisiac, aromatic, prosperous, warming to organs and good for their circulation; to be cinnamon is to increase all appetites (including desire and hospitality), to aid with digestion and reduce blood glucose levels for treating diabetes. Is also to hold violent memories of colonial greed, ripped from the island of Ceylon (Sri Lanka) and patented along with the spice route to symbolize great power for whomever controls its production. But to be cinnamon is also to be a simple, tropical tree, sweet of bark, of such spice for embalming rituals, temple decorations, incense, anointing nuptial hands, bestowing immortality, and when combined with apples, all of the above.
To be bark for the nest of the Phoenix, to be embalmed in a salve of its spice, to warm all the organs simultaneously, to build stamina through the regulation of blood sugars, to hold memories of brutality, to bring lovers together in defiance of borders, to infuse the air with desire, to kiss long and folded in a sweet-scented nest.*

Cinnamon

i.

I should leave but not today,

I try to resist cliché

I can talk quite freely

I cannot talk quite straightly

ii.

Quite often, they return my call

They always call eventually

They think I will continue to desire them but I'm leaving,

I'll never leave,

I'll leave them before they leave me,

Never leave me.

iii.

I sum and total of three: worm, bucket, and cone

They sum total of three plus: solids, boat, shell, and board

iv.

They pound, release, move dangerously towards rock, I take it,

They steal my speech and offer no reassurance

Just block and unblock, veil and flesh, an open and then a closed system

v.

Lift belly, let go through breathing

press, tongue and fold me

then I let them go.

Cinnamon

vi.

Their cinnamon tongue is very alluring,
& conflicts all the stories I have ever been told,
all of the stories I tell them are true, except one:
When I leave, it will be on a Thursday, not unlike today,
Thursday, walking this way, away

When I leave, waters will flow backwards into consciousness,
and forward into flight,
it will be on a Thursday
 not unlike today
just not today.

SHEPHERD'S PURSE

Capsella bursa-pastais

Wispy little white flowers scallop skywards in star-clusters, friend of plantain appearing everywhere especially cracks in sidewalk; resilient when stepped on, bounces right back. Known by many names including Fleur de Saint Jacques, Caseweed, Pick pocket, and Mother's heart, holding knowledge specifically of how to constrict blood vessels, to steady excessive bleeding, to cool the blood, to curb menstrual flooding, to ease the arrival of the crone.

Shepherd's Purse

Sitting snuggly in my belly are seven fibroids,
and my body collapses around their weight.

The blood pours buckets from what is most open in me:
lost babies
loneliness
beauty aging into wisdom…
but not without a fight.

The doctor's words lace surgical scissors into dire predictions;
she speaks sentences that are incised and drained —
she wants to cut them loose.

I seek out the witches.
They feed me nettles and red clover;
shepherd's purse, raspberry leaves and wild yam.
They ask me to see my womb as a bowl filled with water into which is
blooming a singular flower.

They chant:
        ARCH YOUR BACK TO THE FREQUENCY RHYTHM PULSE
              UNIVERSAL LAW OF BELL GONG
    VIBRATION PERFECTION VIBRATION ARCH BACK TONGUE OUT
                  HHHHHHHHHHHHHHHaaaaa
          THE DIVINE UNFOLDS THAT FLOWER ITS ROOTS
                    ABSORB YOUR BLOOD

From the eye of the trance the Goddess,
lion's head and human hands,
drinks wildly the fury of that blood
as it pours down my thighs and straight into her mouth.

Shepherd's Purse

Then, my fibroids,
the whole gaggle of them, start talking:

The first one cackles,
> *I hold the dead, those dear ones you cannot let go of, who are now taking up residence in your womb;*

The second cries,
> *I am carrying shards of rejection that you have wedged snugly down here like slivers of glass hidden among grapes;*

The third is confident,
> *I am bubbling your unexpressed anger into a whirring pool for four, five, and six;*

And the seventh goes straight for my heart—

Finding it broken,
she sets about making a new one,
deep as a root tuned to Earth
pulsed and alive.

GINSENG

Araliaceae

Knotted and sinewy root bearing signatures of human limbs & organs, known to Chinese medicine as "King of Tonics" stimulating yang, building immunity, warming to strengthen stamina in the entire system; known to Indigenous medicines as cooling to calm pain, fevers, digestive troubles, and stop bleeding. As integrating warm & cool, holds great medicinal knowledge simultaneously with the energies of greed and violence which drove fur, gold, and land pillages; 30 tons of ginseng left New York Harbor in 1784 on the first international trade ship bound for China and the profit seeded American independence. Although a protected species in the U.S., still today it is sought by thieves seeking high returns on the black market. Wants to glow and wander around in the night, disguised as a child, luring gatherers to the underworld; would prefer to be gathered at midnight with a wooden spoon.

Ginseng

The night was heavy.
I'd taken care of all the obstacles, but the morning was still a time of dread
when sleep was better spent dreaming than on waking up.
The energy expended was hardly worth the trouble.
I wondered what would wake the sleeper,
and then grew tired of thinking in the dark.

In the morning, deep and crusty, roused from pleasure.
Coming up, pink and ready.
Lap around, a fish in water or two birds of prey.
There is no hesitation when I plunge.
Arrogant, I cut the surface and it breaks in half.
Like the waist of a paper waltz.

An airplane flies low overhead.
There is a triangle of words written in the sky.
The statue stares up at them as if waiting for marching orders.
Upright, as are all tributes to violent men. Bearded or goat-lipped.
They all want to "get down and do it" with the one of their choice,
A moving target who still has no voice.
Still, the subject cannot sit. Still, no context for the scribbles.
Perhaps there is nothing and meaning is merely play.
This story is pretentious and stodgy.
Thicken the plot with ginseng roots, or boil my sound furies.

YARROW

Achillea millefolium

Tall, yellow or white, strong stalked and growing in bushels together abundantly visible in fields, along roadways, and gardens. Holds knowledge of whole-plant medicine in root, stalk, leaves, and flowers, fresh or dried, especially when harvested after a 3-week drought and cut with a black- handed knife. To be yarrow is to stem bleeding and wash wounds, to be "soldier's woundwort" and present for war injuries; also bloodwort, devil's nettle, dog daisy, thousand leaf. To internally induce sweat and break a fever; to accompany witch hazel, bayberry and oakbark as suppository for hemorrhoids; to add to bath and then return to bed; to be smoked along with rosemary and currant leaves in place of tobacco. Also to be I Ching divination sticks, to be wreath over doorways on midsummer's eve and mobile over baby's cradle to keep mal intentions away; to keep witches from entering a house but also giving them clairvoyance; to recall the Hebrides who brush yarrow over eyes to bring second sight and communicate with the dead.

Yarrow

"Yellow," I said, but didn't think he would notice.

I was driving, and the yarrow was growing in a field off the side of the road.

I was right. He didn't notice.

"Huh," he said, as if I was speaking another language. "Never mind, you missed it."

I liked testing him in this way to see if he was really paying attention.

"Pistil," I said, thinking of flowers.

No response.

He continues staring out the window, lost in, whatever, some thought. Maybe the universe. Time.

How everything is connected. And at the same time, falling apart.

Or, maybe just what needed to be done around the house.

"Spackle," I said.

"What?" he said.

"Holes!" I said.

"Oh," he said.

He shook his head and went back to looking out the window.

The sun was setting over the highway, the mosquitoes tapped the windshield with splatter.

Entering into a narrow underpass, the mountains were carved away to make room for a tunnel; we drove right through without blinking.

"I have something to tell you," he said.

I froze. Nouns collapsed into their particle state.

Alone, moving through empty space at 80 miles an hour,

I couldn't hear a thing he was saying.

KUDZU

Pueraria lobata

To be kudzu is to be misunderstood as only being large vines growing from a single rhizome, capable of climbing gigantic trees and blanketing them until they suffocate, and becoming strange shapes. Yet only grows along sunny borders of the forest, like highways where they have an ominous reputation for being invasive, but in reality they don't extend into the forest depths. And are easily mowed down by livestock, and are vulnerable when being eaten by beetles. Some say plants go where they are needed, following humans in an effort to help them. Of roots, effectively used in Chinese medicine to treat alcoholism and relieve hangovers; to treat venous problems and the headache, dizziness, and numbness caused by high blood pressure; to ease leaky gut syndrome, muscle aches, and neck/upper back pain; would prefer to be viewed with more kindness, even as cutting it back from sight.

Kudzu

It started like this:

The suffocating vine and the white moon:
a contrast that made each stand out a little brighter.

The sun drops somewhere, but it's not a part of the narrative.

All this broken nature, she thought.

Surrounded by animals, cloaked by the landscape.

An owl sits on a mound of a world
                                  (roaming through space)
upon which grows a singular tree.

These intersect, he thought to say.

Instead, he told her a story that only made sense in a perfectly ordered universe.
She said: fix your glance on the melting that is actually an emergence.

Is that any way to end a story, he asked?

Is that any way to treat a creature, she replied?

Do you have anything in common with the squirrel, he asked?

Are you alive in your own world but hidden from mine, she replied?

An iceberg teetering off the side of a cliff
    or,

a crow just beyond the frame:

are you somewhere else, he asked?

Kudzu

Outside the rain is pouring down.
The foliage knows only its own rhizome.

Her hesitation made him stop and wonder:
    do things other than green aspire skywards?

In her dream last night, a centipede's legs are a root system supporting the world as we know it

(perfect symmetry, the balance of creation.)

If only she had told him of this vision,

she might have been able to move the ghost that lived between them.

RHUBARB

Rheum rhabarbarum

Stalky, broad, masculine signatures of tall thick stems spilling over, overtaking territory with inviting but poisonous leaves; listen carefully in the dead of night and hear him as he grows. Not the most intelligent of plants, wispy roots barely hold him up, climbing towards the sun and collapsing under the weight. First seeding in China, then named by Greeks **ra barbaron** *meaning "not one of us," the sentiment repeated to describe a ridiculous baseball brawl between players and fans; also repeating "rubarb rubarb rubarb" is how actors create background mumbles, equivalent to blah blah blah, mumbo jumbo, duh duh doon.Still, his pink, red, and white stalks when freshly chopped and added to strawberries in a crumble or pie will aid digestion and move along constipation, and somehow there are boastings that he may have cured the plague.*

Rhubarb

1.

He rings then doesn't.

He determines connection.

He moves through, like imagination does reality.

He scopes and inserts; pours over and behind; rolls.

He reminds planet earth of his presence.

He burns down and finances to build up again.

He leaves the home after building it up.

After roofing, insists on living outside. He commits to history, not memory.

He comes in many colors, but only one pronoun.

He upright, evolutionary, struggling.

He longing for projected ideal; he subconscious lethal.

He imagined as ink stain.

He violence translated back into language.

His internal drives lead to goodness; or war.

He takes inexhaustible pleasure.

He exerts force; his force repressed, anger.

He lies dead on the road; he built the bomb.

He penetrable when gaze circles back.

He in constructing identifies with the rubble.

He in moving rubble cautions the children to be careful where they step.

He impresses with facts and figures.

He refrains from staring even though fashion teeters ass and cleavage.

He victim of violence that is within him.

He holds back but doesn't let go.

What is held back comes through with a vengeance when restricted.

He builds dams to control mighty rivers; then feels bottled up.

He accused of lacking emotion lacks release.

Never allowed to rebel he'll rebel until he's dead.

He mistakes life forces as prolonged adolescence.

Rhubarb

He wakes up and realizes what he has is all he's got.

He disappointed because told early that he could be king of the world.

He always too slow or too quick and can never keep pace with the object of his desire.

He wants to see it all, but upon this seeing has lost the desire that drove him to see in the first place.

He wants his hands all over.

He symbolic order, makes meanings for everyone else.

He complexity, a crossing, is myriad not unlike atom — a collapsing particle.

He spreads, crosses over, supplants one logic with another.

He in a ring, boxing himself silly.

"Murderers!" he hears her cry. "Why kill them? Why not kill yourselves?"

He is beauty and inertia; the balloon caught by the chimney's grate.

He bombs, calls it caring; erases, calls it freedom.

Occupies through want of love; destroys when love is reciprocated.

THYME

Thymus vulgaris

First seeded in Eurasia, of mint, as remedy for all kinds of acute infections, especially related to lung, stomach, and urinary tract; when combined with fenugreek, clears sinus congestion; when combined with wild cherry bark, eases coughs and colds; when combined with chamomile as tea taken before bed, eases nightmares. Of connecting to dream worlds to call forth a lover, or to stuff into a dream pillow to remember dreams in the morning. Of aromatic and sacred, regal and humble, of purifying sacred space and, when added to baths, boosting of courage or purging of accidental poisoning; of being planted in coffins and around graves. Sudden whiffs of aroma indicate a ghost is present. A sprig brushed across the eyes sees ghosts and fairies. Among carpets sweet & plush, bees abound and grazing chickens wander.

Thyme

the speckled hen is and what matters most in this area of —
rooster, she said my husband is —
magically in tune with what matters most —
here we are and now that you mention it —
out loud I might say, "I don't know what you are saying" —
I feel fine not knowing I don't know what —
comes of it? what comes of —

going inward without that realization that outward is —

thyme, that's what the chickens eat

fragrant, sprawling mattering as what else? what else?

a bird sitting on an aromatic stool, waiting.

RASPBERRY

Rubus strigosus

On the brambles of Mt. Ida the nymph Ida scratched her breast/pricked her finger/brushed up against thorny brambles while tending to her child, staining the white fruits red. Now many varieties spreading and cultivating all over the world, and everywhere the medicinal power of manganese-rich raspberry has been used as a tonic for women to help control menstrual irregularities, oxygenate the cells, strengthen the blood, and support pregnancy by soothing labor pains and relaxing the uterus to ease contractions. A tonic and strengthener connecting female energies to Venus and the moon; also to wear as a garland to tame bewitched horses. Gathers in the toes and scat of bear who love to frolic in her thicket and then travel far and wide, spreading seeds wherever the wind blows.

Raspberry

I imagined
from those woods
a clearing through raspberry brambles
where that snarly bear guards her cubs
and I imagined you with your knife
breaking her twice:
once with a cut from throat to vulva
and once with the slight tremor of your heart
which — animal that you are —
gave her a moment of hope
that instead of mounting
her you would
take her in.
Offer her shelter.
Lie with her still as the poetry
She must write to live.

DEAD NETTLE

Lamium purpureum

To grow amongst dandelions in early spring, to cover ground with soft purple stalked flowers, to hold upside down and see a couple, in bed, and so to heal rifts between lovers; to be a charm, to offer protection to the house and good storage for the fairies who put their shoes in each of the tiny stacked flowers. To partner well with plantain as a topical salve, to ease bug- bites and draw the purple out of bruises. To be loved by pollinating bees and butterflies in meadows of symbiotic delight.

Dead Nettle

He reassured me the sun is safe and his wings are stealth;
His feathers are a skin of radar-absorbent material, steel buckles,
aerodynamic restraints.
He will be suspended but moving upward with calm velocity.

I stayed behind in the trailer which he had parked close to a deer crossing
marked by a field of dead nettle.
He taught me to shoot; I had plenty to forage.
He told me that when the propane tank is empty and the lamplight goes
out, I should look into the sky to see a star that is not a star:
That's me, he said. I'm coming home.

When he returned, he was badly burned.
When he returned, every organ was pierced by solar arrows.
He was terrified of fire and refused to ignite the pilot light.
He gnashed his teeth and snarled at me when I told him I was cold.
Woman, he said, if you think you are cold then go to where the sun does
not shine.
I'm still waiting for him to come home.

The woods are dark and the last of the snow has melted.
Icicles drop from tall pines and pierce the ground.
I see him falling, everywhere.

AMARYLLIS

Hippeastrum equestre

Originally seeding in South Africa and capturing the heart of Virgil, who tells of the love stricken Amaryllis who consulted the oracle of Delphi for a spell to win over the heart of the handsome but shy shepherd Alteo, who lived alone in a field of exquisite flowers; she was instructed to stand outside of his house and pierce her own heart repeatedly with a golden arrow. After doing this for 30 days, flowers blossomed from her spilled blood, and the shepherd was indeed smitten; he named the flowers "Amaryllis" and they lived among her glorious, fertile, producing, verisimilitude: clown, picotee, ruby star, desire, apple blossom, red peacock, dancing queen, snow drift. nymph. Youthful lovesickness carries an antidote, for she is sister of the Belladonna lily, and equally poisonous if ingested; while dying, the flower moistens and exudes a rich dark red ink which, like pokeberry, can be used to transcribe dreams, bind treaties, concoct spells, dye cotton, and see the future.

Amaryllis

i.

now that you are here
in the future
I will have needed to leave
many things behind
to be with you here
in this moment
time-gapped falling plunge-long
wall-less space
time radical rupture and divide
you are a pronoun, disappearing
flare candles neural twitches spinal response
congregate flaring quelled by looking
sequestered freshkills disappearing
memory lights screen seeping blue ceiling
sleeping into morning thought evolving
mirror moon howling
prophesies of our immortality

ii.

I remember holding you actually
holding the space around you
you held tightly even more so from afar
I tighten us grasping
stay with me here
just a little while longer
or leave me to not keep holding
lest I become, otherwise
meaning lost incomprehensively to screens

Amaryllis

iii.
no more projecting let's just fall in love
no more driving slowly
no more shrinking the amaryllis
flowers where we lie

APRICOT

Prunus armeniaca

Called melon, malum, apple and precocious; origin seeding is uncertain – Armenia, India, China. Sweet, sweet fruit rolls into thin sheets (Syria and Egypt); vitamin rich seeds used to treat asthma, coughs, and constipation; of seductive signature resembling luscious skin foldings (French: abricot); brings bodies together borderless, playful, nutritious, delicious, gentle fruit to roll off the tongue and then kiss your lover. Sister of apple, whose origin in antiquity encompassed all sweet fruit.

Apricot

oyster

apricot

lychee artichoke

folds

sticking sweetly bunly rolled

like tootsie hard bit down chew

stickily orange apple round stemmed wormholes rooted

round soft spots licking hungrily the jolly and the rancher

completely surrender to the night

beauty bound into a fractal of bedpost

sheetless as every shore contains the totality of sand

dunes spacetime in potential

a collision of commas

we know what to do with these bodies

tuned to cosmic pulses

stars born, neurons fired

universe banged and bucked

night eternally repeated

totally sourced

sound surrounds

eclipses of the moon go on forever

when groundless

we are lost to the world

screenless

ST. JOHN'S WORT

Hypericum perforatum

Yellow flowers growing low but proud along roadsides, prefers southern facing slopes and open fields, not deep dark woods, lifts spirits. For wounds inside and out, restores lifeforce, calms thoughts, reminds that life is long. Nests under pillows to drive away evil spirits, roots surface on Midsummer's Eve and burn in bonfires to boost the fire's intent; smoke cleanses spaces and boosts ritual energies. Oil dabbed on amulets boosts the power of love charms. As nervine offers energy to depression and anxiety; regulates the solar plexus and eases insomnia; is a powerful anti-viral to help wounds and infections including shingles, mono, and the flu. Bringer of magic to ease fears of abandonment or failure, restorer of harmony between mind and body, dissipater of energy vampires lurking in houses, especially those that threaten sanity.

St. John's Wort

Water running.

Occasionally the pipes rattle. Doors slam. The environment is alive.

No wonder sleeping is so difficult. Outside, kids are screaming hello.

So excited to see each other. Why does it always come to this?

The squawking of what sounds like a very large and angry crow.

A chair pulling back against the tile.

Hangers rustling in the room next door.

Minute things become worthy of words.

Parallel universes exist, no doubt about it.

St. John's Wort

Whistle blowing somewhere.

Wood behind the desk with two thumbtacks.

Possibility of attaching important documents (yet to be determined).

Everyone's watches are set the same.

Everyone knows what they know and have always believed. Clock. Machinery. Socket.

Occasional bird songs.

If I stand in the middle of the circle I hear an echo.

An intriguing notion: logic falls apart when I am alone in the room.

St. John's Wort

Someone else is running.

A man's voice is trying to attract another man who is yelling.
Things get so confusing.

Outside I know there is a dark entryway that allows men to access the boiler.

It is a very manly hallway, because it is dark, and because it serves no other function except to get to the boiler.

I wouldn't go there.

All I can think about is who is hiding there.

Who is going to pull me in.

Whereas a man looking at that space would think, "that's a good clearance for the boiler."

St. John's Wort

Now, an even angrier crow. He is in bed.

He's thinking that the "caw caw" in the middle of the night is a squawking bird.

I know it is a machine. I hear it differently.

I hear the patterns, the repetitions, the recession of space between the squawks.

He hears the squawks getting louder when, he assumes, the large bird is angry or vying for some attention.

He says there is not a pattern to the sounds. I hear the pattern, loud and clear.

I'm sure it is a machine.

Funny, this thing about walls.

St. John's Wort

Something did happen, actually. But not to me.

Besides, I know too much about it. Anyway, I can't spill the beans.

Because all I can do is sit here and listen. The heater has just activated.

Now I know it is the heater.

Yesterday I actually thought someone was intentionally banging on the pipes just to scare me.

I thought the same thing about the refrigerator turning on with a big eruption.

And I thought the same thing about an unidentified sound which at first sounded like a footstep.

I now realize it was a squirrel somewhere in the walls.

Really, the house doesn't scare me anymore.

ROSE

Rosa

Rose gall, rose marrow, hibiscus, rose of China, rose of Sharon, rose of winter, rosin rose, rose haw. Behind a left ear helps find a lover, behind a right helps keep one, behind both beckons another. When darkened and brittle, cast a spell; find hibiscus growing at a crossroads and don't touch it lest you be possessed; place a picture of roses on your desk to inspire creative inspiration. Dog rose, beach rose, dagger rose, pixy pears, wild briar, witches briar, sweet briar rose, eglantine rose. Line roads with petals for festival days, scatter petals over the graves of loved ones, dust petals with sugar and crumble into brandy. Charms against sorcery and protects against thunder and lightning, elves and dwarves. Rosehips as garland or necklace protects; splash oil of rose on skin or rub on lips; pulp out of fruit mixed with sugar quenches thirst and cools fever. Rich in bioflavonoids and vitamin C, fruits strengthen capillaries; uplifting, stress reducing, hopes to heal heartache.

Rose

Covet not another's except sex them
if ever you are alone at this feast
there will be deer for dinner,
roses for true love,
or not, depending on who's coming.
Because Hudson stars are heaving themselves ecstatic
and love songs are fractals moving into infinity,
what is everything else, anyway?
Not block but its opposite, crystal.
Not despair but its opposite, blossom.
We hear the same stories many times
and still repeat the boring ending,
the one with the cellar.
Now why would you ever want to go back there?

DANDELION

Taraxacum officinale

To be dandelion is to be misunderstood, as companion to grass but perceived as weed although every part of the yellow flowering plant is medicine; greens for salad or soup, roots tinctured as blood purifier to treat liver toxicity, flowers to assimilate nutrients and eliminate bile, minerals to clear and aid organs in their elimination of toxins; brings wishes, invites gentle blows to loosen parachute being-seeds, fairies in disguise, catch one for luck and whisk away aggressive energies. To be a yellow flower changing to white, whimsical seed-fairy overnight, to spiral with the wind and travel far and wisely, spreading deep knowledge. Resilient, regenerative, cooperative, systemic, non- hierarchal generative beings; hard to uproot once seeded, so why bother.

Dandelion

A gust, cups, seeds, clouds,

amethyst, buckweed burns like sun, nervous & ready for the beach, till the ceiling falls, in bed maybe, the smoke clear light, walls cave in comets to blame, deep suffering, mundane shock make it right, come on, correct things, sob story, tattered tape, rice crackers and cakes, helmet? hornet's nest? boats snap braincase loose, lineaments of ash, cloth closing in, due to silence we stayed together, though quite worn through and bundled, blow things up like wacky adhesive dried in drive-through shakes, silence brings unwanted guests, someone blow it into the wind or bring on brewskies.

In a hunch the lawns outside burst into yellow fields of dandelion

golden source, cusp a corpse, I will tell you what to do, pull surface moisture from skin, grotesque sweating, soul strong as daylight, centipede twitches, salt slug, rosy featured, grass as a pointer all from one hand, dull, cowards, I know to survive, blood in the vortex, fixed on futurity, eyes growing darker, hard lived lessons, voice gone scratchy, browbeaten blizzard, bullets whiz, brightness wishes, seeds spread.

ROSEMARY

Rosmarinus officinalis

Holds memory as sacred to many cultures, as maintaining connections between the living and the dead, as placed in graves and carried down the mourning path, as growing in the garden, as keeping the house safe from witches, lightning, and fairies. "The herb of remembrance" hung above beds remembers dreams and integrates difficult memories of the past; opens space in the mind for difficult memories to surface with refreshed insight. Improves circulation to the brain, helps headaches, and oxygenates blood vessels, especially when combined with wintergreen, willow bark, and licorice. Strengthens the stomach, expels wind, removes obstructions in the liver; helps with digestion and hair washing when combined with yarrow leaves & southernwood.

Rosemary

Un(theory)conscious: buriedmemory
between "lost" and
"recollect" comes
incomplete encounter
with the un(loss)dead
with some past event,
never c(overcome)mpletely,
nor adequately rem(trauma)embered
vague but incomplete connection
to some past event
"filling in"
with other memories
so as to not adequately
(dis)remem-(placement)ber

Rosemary

Unconscious is absolut(otal)e memory,
indestructible-potential-effective-virulent
"In mental life nothing which has once been formed can perish...
everything is somehow preserved...
and in suitable circumstances...
it can once more be brought to light" (Freud).

Remem(ber)-brance is re(cure)onstruct the "rubble"
of past(foundation)event, the rem(iniscences)nants.
Symptoms manifest in the bo(mala)dy
and remembering is the bringing-to-consciousness of "un(lost)-conscious"
to active remem(hybrid)brance.

This process is often called "working through" lim(loss)bo:
neither total remembrance,
nor total loss or forgetting, rather
a hy(between)brid memory & loss.

The un(active)conscious
is the body is everyday existence
is quan(systemic)titatively the larger part,
now see an unbidden image:
riding bareback on a wild horse

Rosemary

Reminis(ghosts)cences are like

the "un(horror)dead"
neither completely

dead(haunt)alive
seeking resolution.

This is why symp(pain)toms
(migraines, frequent headaches)
are clogged with stagnant memory
and have a subtly seething

impact on our existence.

RED CLOVER

Trifolium pratense

Abundantly, spontaneously, growing in meadows, fields and along roadsides, as light and dark reddish tubular small petals cascade into roundish bundles, as friend to butterflies, ants, bees, and fairy folk. As high in vitamins, minerals, and isoflavones, as holding knowledge of being a sweet tasting blood purifier and female-body estrogen balancing tonic; as aiding menopausal women to help inhibit estrogen-dependent cancers and stave off bone loss, especially when combined with other roots and herbs. A wash for skin eruptions of psoriasis and eczema, also spreads knowledge of love, money, protection and luck. Holds so much simultaneously so as to clarify vision and allow painful memories to surface and be held by the perennial wisdom of ancestors, the meadow, and the field.

Red Clover

The road of long middles is traveled by tortoises who move scattering syntax—they don't care about telling a story with a beginning, middle, and end. They collect words on their feet and tread them through the red clover, leaving droppings on passing landscapes of forest, field, and asphalt.

Into the long middle we roam, talking of death and love as twin flames tamed as circulation, migration, circumnavigation
even as we build walls and enclosures to keep everything contained.

The house on my back: lights laundry dog packed up to the walker daughter packed up to school drive one way drive the other way make calls do dishes make shake make coffee take train teach stop sit.
Meditate. Breathe. Relax.
Repeat.
Run as fast as you can.

"Run as fast as you can."
I drop into that sentence to the place in my body where it is all tangled up
the way a fishing line catches a child who is taking up
a lot of space trying to swim against the current, not seeing herself
as inchoate
and yet she is crying rivers to rock her sleep

Red Clover

Spiraling:
daughter confused by mother who tells father all the things daughter does wrong, even though father blames mother for everything that goes wrong. "Systemic empathy." Will it be enough to disembarrass?

The field between bodies created when we are in the same room together is ancestral trauma, is trying to breathe, is calling forth stories to be understood in the space between

Do you feel that you are a part of something? Do you feel that you belong? The first step is to include the past

The secret life of breathing holds a collective consciousness where EVERYbody belongs and noONE is excluded

Red Clover

: Energy must fulfill itself :
Meaning that trauma gets further entangled, gets bigger and bigger, as all who have been excluded take up residence in their living ancestors as energy not fulfilled, flailing wildly as a child is drawn to that unfinished energy, thinking she can fix it but

she sees the rose brittle long before she breaks

Wonders: what do I have to do to belong????????
What do I have to give??????
What can I take without my parents going completely berserk??????
How do I get the hell out of this tangle???????

Hold on, everybody, a healing is trying to take place:
hold the image of each person in their place of belonging
holding the story turtles tell

Red Clover

that stillness is golden, that golden is silence, that silence is a word, that the word is a wish, that the wish is a berry, that the berry is plenty, that plenty is the cup and the juice filled it amply, that the water is cool, that cool is a cloth, that the cloth is silk, that the silk wraps the pain, that the pain can breathe, that the breath is a tree, that the tree has roots, that roots are passageways, that the ants are home, that the leaves are nourishment, that the green is cellular, that cellular is cosmic, that the cosmic is starlight, that the dust is falling, on the crown, in the eyes, into the palm, then scattered through time, to the generations, to the ancestors, to the turtles, wandering is such stillness.

FRANKINCENSE

Botswellia carterii

Of Boswellia sacra, of endangered trees, first seeding in the driest of climates, Oman, Yemen, Eritrea, Ethiopia, Somalia, Sudan, India, gifts of the Magi, and holder of ancient ceremonies. The intense perfume comes from the dried resin of bark, the "tears" of the cuts. Holds incense route memories of colonization as used to fuel the economic engine of empires; now would like to be left alone. Holds ritual memories of fragrant smoke to facilitate contact with the deity to whom it is presented; to fumigate divinatory mirrors so the witch can behold the truth, to hide the scent of the dead, to mark ritual circles, to bring forth past lives.

Frankinscense

A shape evolved outside of your somnambulistic twitches, like an aura but not multi-colored.
Maybe call it a blueprint,
a coming-out into angelic form of some unique configuration of genes and proteins,
amino acids and neurotransmitters (a complex process) moving into a cosmic origami

I might have thought it was beautiful, for a moment,
But this blueprint took on a different shape from the organism (you) that made it grow.
A shape, in other words, with no previous mold, a shaky and not at all quiet kind of thing.
The question is how, and of whose design?
Or maybe the opposite is the question: whose randomness?

When it finished evolving, the monstrous became cellular, particular, and infiltrated
(meaning, at the heart of everything).
Once built, it commanded attention,
took over territories and planted flags,
wanted blood and with every drop, it evolved

Demanded to be observed and replicated,
the way of screens, no longer strange.

ASPEN

Populus Tremuloides

Extensive root systems of suckers seeking to shoot through tree groves and entwine with pine, fir, hemlock, maple, birch, and alders. Ancient, quaking one of many seeds who lives 150-200 years. Rod of aspen, fé, measures newly dug graves to ensure snug fit of the occupant; crossed branches atop hallowed ground keeps suspected witches under; twigs placed on an altar will connect to ancestors; ashes scattered around trunk allows spirits to find company among roots and canopies. Like willow, bark contains salicin, the main component of aspirin; soothes aches and pains of humans, bears, elk, beavers, grouses, and quail. Rustling sounds golden; standing amongst the hummmm calms the mind, connects with dead loved ones, and allows whatever is ready to surface to come through.

Aspen

hummmm & what else is there what else stopbreathe

●

        breathbreathbreathspace   space

                                           breathe

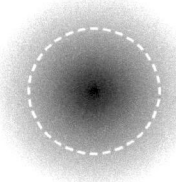 m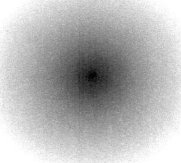

grove m space between m

        arched door through trees sway

feelingspacebreath m

                m space

                                space breath m

Aspen

and we are— here now— what happens
when/if the occurrence of feeling
    a blank— a day at a time

see how that is why I
    in this moment know what it
    means—

now to notice— all the parts are
    present here

Aspen

                  as are you present here
           what sound is that & in what language
—do I know—know better than   this
                      place—

not through sight but will get around to speaking clearly,

                      even so

Aspen

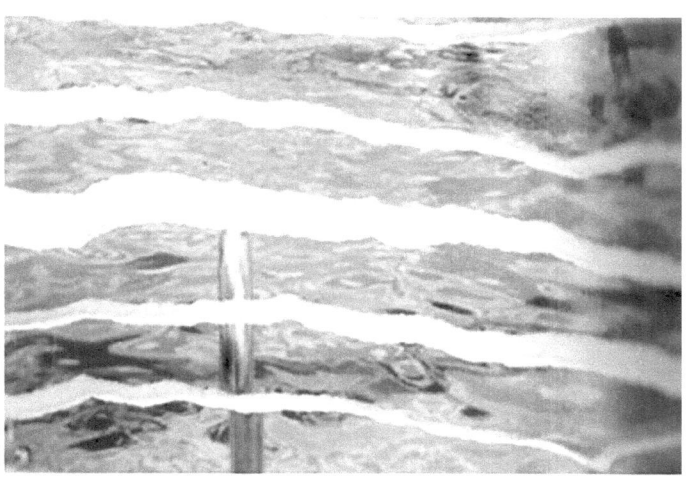

then the choosing   — which is real?
        — unaware how spoken things happen,
       or don't depending on their syntax —
      I felt the emergence and noticed the roots —
        shoot out of nowhere but written —
         talked but not out of mind,
       rather out of gap-in-thought-spot —
         here now, on&off flickers
          everything else — as song
     or dance and sing? make rain noises?
…as if I could be anything other than shape, shaper, shaping, shaped —
anything other than continuity, fluid, flow,
       &changing m

LOBELIA

Lobelia cardinalis

Cascading tubular bright red flowers with long thin petals supported by strong thick stalk and leaves. Kin to boneset, grounds indigenous wisdom to ease spasms in body and constrictions in skeletal muscles. Profound intelligence reads the overall vital force of a body and orients itself towards the organ or system that seek its relaxant effects; travels to the precise destination where it is most needed: asthma, cramping, passing of kidney and gall bladder stones. FDA deems it poisonous because if taken in too large quantities it will induce, vomiting, and partial paralysis. Unlike pharmaceutical disclaimers, certain symptoms are actually a part of the healing process and unlikely to be lethal.

Lobelia

i.

swirl symptoms not as a projection into the bodies that reflect and surround you, but into the pattern, the channel, the stream and the river, the one where you too are in relation, struggling to survive, where we all are, there, where we all are, there, the most difficult part is not knowing how, where I am, hiding, I see you as you see me where the sun never shines, where the trees are, the beetle-infested trees, you down there, where we all go — to the beneath where underground we lay, and all who suffer are there too, your trauma to cut the end of cause and effect, breathing, why do we inflict such harm on each other, such cruelty, to the animals, to each other, why breathing do we spiral time backwards where the vortex is spinning us into sync with waves and fire, we destroyed our species just to return to where we had been all along, why

I loved you there, the wind, I always will, I will see you there again,

                    will I?

Lobelia

ii.

all sentences end in cherries, all dogs that curl in puddles, all flowers
grow precisely aslant to angle birdsong, all red lobelia ink-stain to
water pen's pocket, to charmed amulet trance, to dance green magenta
contradictions, to fatigue out of candles removed, to sync with music,
to mosquito tutelage, acorn lessons, solstice attention, sorrowful breeze,
eyes foot reflex, trance fixations, dreaming of floating into objects &
finding talismans of deepest desires, crusted bark rings hidden in
the trunks of trees where branches reach towards the sky, the space
between the sky is blue, that's entranced vision, floating up there,
above it all, looking down through peripheral vision, eyes, feeling breath
coming only when floating, coming through big toe tip catching, coming
through visionary tics and the vibrating photons of interplanetary light

as neurons ignite a-synchronic symphonies.

PINE

Pinaceae

Of the fibronchi sequence & fractal pattern that forms the organizing consciousness of nature & life itself; in this way is kin to sunflower, lichen, and rose. Cosmic portal when hung as wreath on door for winter solstice to welcome the return of light. Concentrates psychic work and when drawn as a circle in the air stimulates defensive energies and breaks hexes. White pine bark (pinus strobus) expectorates mucus and fights infections especially chronic bronchitis; pine gum for wound healing; pine pollen to strengthen muscles and tendons, pinecone jam on morning toast for stability and strength. Ballads exhault knowledge of a child lost in the pines, exposed to dangers beyond her understanding.

.

Pine

tune chair to pitchforks

drop water into mind at play

digitally remaster sandbox to fit only one way

look out while wondering as dog barks let me in

warm tea as wandering hem skirts kale crumbs

avoid withstanding another's outside;

withstanding anchor to self

drop tantrums into heart center

dissipate wandering eardrums

make love to candlelight avoid wax

when in mind of winter be like pine

WILD CHERRY

Prunus avium

Kin to rose, plum and peach. Family tree includes over 125 species of which 17 reach tree size in western hemisphere. Flowering five pinkish to white petals, sometimes becoming rounded fruits of juicy pulp around compressed stone (inside the stone is the seed). Offers all parts as nourishment and hospitality for animals, birds, and humans. Calming to respiratory nerves, soothing for cough and asthma, collaborates with cramp bark, lobelia, ginger and honey as sweet syrup to expel phlegm, ease mucus membranes, and normalize histamine reactions; quelling for mental restlessness & agitation; relaxing for seduction. Witches Broom Disease infects branches causing dense, broomlike tufts where no fruit grows – offerings of libations and drumming in orchards pacify evil spirits' efforts to prevent blooming. Burning bark keeps witches away, a pile of stones attracts romance, and blossoms in a bride's bouquet keep hope eternal.

Wild Cherry

I spend my days

Listening to humans

Talk about transforming

What it means to be human

In the realm of lack

We say how will it be to be

Without anxiety

Without triggers

Without insomnia

Without dread

Without always feeling that dull kind of crying

Waterless

Paced

No ambition

No hope

No attachment

To anything that passes the time

And anyone who might need love.

It would be easier

To be human

On top of a mountain

Alone with the goats

Who roam satisfied

Eating the bark

Just me and the smoke

Of my little fire

Speck to the satellite

Microbe to the pandemic

Wild Cherry

Whoever said this human thing
Is some kind of connection
To divine consciousness

As if that
Were anywhere to park

But here we all are, anyway.
Birthed from the Goddesses' thigh
And then swallowed whole
Incubating in her nebula
Sailing through space.

SAGE

Salvia officinalis

Grows the earth all over, finds sacred place with indigenous wisdoms to burn and use for protection, also holds medicine memory of how to treat colds and fever, cool night sweats, induce perspiration, soothe hoarse throat and laryngitis, ease nerves. In the company of fire will heighten concentration to connect with spirit guides and focus clairvoyance for psychic work. Flows urine and stimulates kidneys, cleanses dandruff, cools ulcers and sores, promotes longevity, honors the dead. Settles grief's pain and anger when planted in graves, remedies a broken heart's fear of never being loved again when carried as an amulet.

Sage

The poet says:

Close your eyes and see the location of something
or someone you have lost, including yourself.
Remove all nouns from the vision:
darkhollowwooden-likeburied

Float above the sentence,
open your eyes and look in front of you,
at what is actually there()here,
remove (again) all nouns from your vision and write
into the space of what is left behind:
greenedgeblurlineswalking blacknesswhitenessurrounds
perpendicularstacks asideslanted
backwardblows stillmoves
The poet says:
Here(there) is where you will find heshetheyyouit
or something
(elsefloating into landscape)
you have been looking for but didn't know you were looking

signopposites starwrist wormwooddrip greenlayers
greenonyellow(blowing)
plantspresent(as)cellstars((exploding))
curvedtilts
fall not confused
inability thoughtedge onebody endsanother
begins ohlove of sagesprigrootsystem

Sage

confusion is edgebody tightaction collapse backward
stopping(sucking) universeballcurves
trees(love)magneticcycles

potentialvision
stilldoor waywhite wall turnaslant stasis
motionpotential plotwobbles timemoves
mindsignals animalsberriesleafsways
motionstilldancing
roots(mycelium[web]connect)foreshadow
newgrowthtocome

spacepulled intime(intimacy)
pentothought gravitybody
cellularshifts
selfdestructpower(less)abuse absolute
plantmedicines(thank you for)helping(me)
swiftmovingcurrent
plotthickening room lightswift
cover(covert)quiet poisedmotion

cusp(plot) touching(cusp)
almostbutnotquiteyet (mean)ing
calmeyestorm
mindquiet racingnothing denouement(plotdrop)
barkbudblossom

ritual quiettime healspirals
red candle, white candle, paper & pen, metal tin & matches
drinktea()quietspace

Sage

The poet says:
Circle protect me(others)&earth
plantsanimalscreatures
from energies I cannot help but to release;
cannot carry or hold,
can(must)not pass down
or transmit to
daughteranimalsotherstreesplantsmeadows

holdpaperhandscandle
chant, shout, screamsounds
rage into redwax burns
rage into whitewax burns
brighterhotter(force)angerfuels
firepaperashes
release (down) circleenergy earthsink
thankelements watching over me thank
fractalseeds earthmeadow bodyalive sleepcandles()out

ashes to all violent acts of speech & harm & aggression you have experienced or inflicted consciously(unconsciously)ancestrally ashes to all you have experienced/are experiencing in the world consciously or ancestrally are holding/have held ashes

PROVENANCE AND CITATIONS

Unless otherwise noted, the *materia medica* (plant descriptions) are compiled from the following books: *The Occult Family Physician and Botanic Guide to Health* by Mrs. Antonette Matteson, Trance and Healing Medium (Buffalo, NY: 1894); *Medicinal and Other Uses of North American Plants: A Historical Survey with Special Reference to the Eastern Indian Tribes* by Charlotte Erichsen-Brown (Dover, 1979); *Field guide to North American Trees* by Thomas Elias (Grolier, 1989); *The Way of Herbs* by Michael Tierra (Pocket Books, 1990); *The Modern Herbal Dispensatory: A Medicine Making Guide* by Thomas Easley and Steven Horne (North Atlantic Books, 2016); *The Witches Encyclopedia of Magical Plants* by Sandra Kynes (Llewellyn Publications, 2024). Additional sources for individual plants are cited below.

Preamble

"Learning the Grammar of Animacy" in *Braiding Sweetgrass: Indigenous Wisdom, Scientific Knowledge, and the Teachings of Plants* by Robin Wall Kimmerer, Milkweed Editions, 2020. p. 48-59. Thanks to Kythe Heller and the Language&Thinking Workshop at Bard College where this prompt was initially conceived.

Anise

Additional source: The Star Anise Peace Project:
[https://gist2017.weebly.com/esthers-blog/planting-seeds-of-hope-through-the-star-anise-peace- project-in-myanmar]

Slippery Elm

Published in two earlier versions: first as "String Tracks: after Helmut Federel's 'Structures of Deviance, Blue Sisters series of 10 etchings'" in

Traverse, edited by Drew Kunz & Stacy Szymaszek, Spring 2002; subsequently revised as "Old Human, New Consciousness" for the anthology *Poetics for the More than Human World*, edited by Mary Newell, Sarah Nolan and Bernard Quetchenbach, Spuyten Duyvil Press, 2020.

Boneset

"Bones" is interpreted by Nora Babalan and Timbala on their album "Sadza with the Head of a Mouse," 2018 [https://timbila.bandcamp.com/ album/sadza-with-the-head-of-a-mouse-mouse]. *Additional source*: "Joe Pye, Joe Pye's Law,and Joe-Pye-Weed: The History and Eponymy of the Common Name Joe-Pye-Weed for Eutrochium Species (asteraceae)" by Richard B. Pearce and James S. Pringle. *The Great Lakes Botanist*, Volume 56, Issue 3-4, 2017, p. 177-200 [https:// quod.lib.umich.edu/m/mbot/0497763.0056.303/2/--joe-pye-joe-pyes-law-and-joe-pye-weed-the-history?page=root;size=100;view=image]

Sunflower

Published as "Still Above: shadowing Samuel Beckett's 'Act Without Words,'" in the chapbook *Emulation Etudes*, edited by Richard Deming and Nancy Kuhl, Phylum Press, 2010.
Additional source: "Circadian regulation of sunflower heliotropism, floral orientation, and pollinator visits" [https://zenodo.org/records/889822]

Poke

Published as "Tales for Caw: from a line by Ammiel Alcalay" in *Jacket 32*, April 2007.

Pomegranate

Published as "Orphee" for a broadside accompanied by a collage by George Schneeman, edited by Gary Parrish, Farfalla Press/McMillan &

Parrish, 2006; subsequently published in *Sidebrow* #1, 2008.

Additional source: "A Secret, Symbolic History of Pomegranates" by Kate Lebo [https://lithub.com/a-secret-symbolic-history-of-pomegranates/]

Plantain

Published as "Upside Down," *Marsh Hawk Review*, Fall 2008. Revised as "Still Life," *Colorado Review*, edited by Matthew Cooperman, (Issue 37.3) 2010.

Additional source: *Braiding Sweetgrass: Indigenous Wisdom, Scientific Knowledge, and the Teachings of Plants* by Robin Wall Kimmerer, Milkweed Editions, p. 212-215; "The ubiquitous plantain" by Susan Albert [https://susanalbert.com/plant-lore-garden-mysteries-and-herbal-magic]

Nettle

Titled "No Cure: Shadowing T.S. Eliot" and published in my book *Everywhere Here and in Brooklyn: A Four Quartets*, Belladonna Collaborative, 2012.

Additional source: "Native American Stinging Nettle Mythology" [http://www.native-languages.org/legends-nettle.htm]

Holly

Published as "Blackbird: homage to Kenneth Rexroth's poem 'The blackbird sings and the baby laughs midway in the century of horror,'" *The Chicago Review: Kenneth Rexroth special issue*, Autumn 2007.

Additional source: "Holly: Legends, Customs, and Myths," [https://exten- sion.psu.edu/holly-legends-customs-and-myths]

Geranium

Originally published as "Another Century" in *The Colorado Review* edited by Matthew Cooperman, (Issue 37.3), 2010, 136-137.

Additional sources: "A historical, scientific and commercial perspective on the medicinal use of Pelargonium sidoides (Geraniaceae)." [https://www.sciencedirect.com/science/article/abs/pii/S0378874108004054; botanical drawings: https://casabio.org/BOOKS/PELARGONI-UMS-SOUTHERN-AFRICA]

Mugwort

References: Rilke, Rainer Marie from "The First Elegy" of *Duino Elegies*, translated by Stephen Mitchell, Shambhala Publications, 1992. Also referred to here is a ritual led by Anaiya Sophia, a self-ordained "divinized sexuality coach" to work with the aggression and rage at having been forced to silence one's expression. "There is a point at which women have cut themselves off from their own bodies and their own sexuality, the place where we have turned all these acts of sexual violence and uncon- sciousness against ourselves." [https://anaiyasophia.com/]

Feverfew

Additional source: [https://astonishinglegends.com/astonishing-leg-ends/2019/3/30/feverfew-folklore]

Hawthorn

published as "t h r o u g h o u t s i d e" in Salt, edited by Billie Chernoff, *Lunar Chandelier Press*, 2021.

Holy Basil

Published as "Fallen Left Behind: Shadowing Charles Simic's 'Elegy'" in UrVox (Issue 2), 2002. Subsequently published as "Voices Variously Heard" in my book I, *Afterlife: Essay in Mourning Time*, Essay Press, 2007. *Additional source*: [https://usbasilconsortium.rutgers.edu/all-about-basil/basil-history-and-culture/]

Aloe
Published as "Windowless" in *Barrow Street*, edited by Peter Covino, Barrow Street Press, Summer 2005. Subsequently appears in *A Waiting Room Reader* edited by Rachel Hadas, Cavan Kerry Press, 2013.

Arnica
Additional source: "La Sauvage Arnica: ethnobotanique" [https://herboris- teriepaysanne.fr/la-sauvage-arnica-ethnobotanique/]

Mandrake
Originally titled "I will think about my lover's body and free myself of desire" after a passage by Chögyam Trungpa: "You are taught that in order to free your mind of desire that you should reflect on the different parts of your lover's body, thinking of it in terms of flesh, bones, mucus, hairs, internal organs, and so forth. However, although that approach might have worked at one time, in modern times it is problematic. Highly accomplished physicians know the body inside out; nonetheless, they do not stop falling in love. Working with desire is not all that simple." Chögyam Trungpa, excerpt "Cutting Ego Fixation" from *The Bodhisattva Path of Wisdom and Compassion*, edited by Judith Lief. Copyright © 2013 by Diana Mukpo. Reprinted by arrangement with The Permissions Company, LLC on behalf of Shambhala Publications Inc., Boulder, Colorado, shambhala.com.

Cinnamon
Homage to "Black Stone on a White Stone" by César Vallejo.

Shepherd's Purse
Published as "What the Fibroid Said" in *Stained: An Anthology of Writing About Menstruation*, Querencia Press, 2022.

Ginseng

Originally published as "Red" in *Downtown Brooklyn: A Journal of Writing #9, 2000*; subsequently published as *Red*, a chapbook edited by Mary Burger, Second Story Press, 2001; subsequently translated by Sandra Moussempes and published in *Action Poétique*, Spring 2003.

Additional source: "The Mysterious Powers of American Ginseng" by Astrid Stephenson, *Smithsonian Center for Folklife & Cultural Heritage*, March 27, 2019

[https://folklife.si.edu/magazine/mysterious-medicinal- economic-powers-american-ginseng]

Yarrow

Published as "Yellow" in *The Review of General Semantics*, Institute for General Semantics, Spring 2021.

Kudzu

Additional source: "The True Story of Kudzu, the Vine That Never Truly Ate the South" by Bill Finch.

[https://www.smithsonianmag.com/sci- ence-nature/true-story-kudzu-vine-ate-south-180956325/]

Rhubarb

Additional source: "The etymology of the word rhubarb" by Sam Dean.
[https://www.bonappetit.com/test-kitchen/ingredients/article/the-etymol- ogy-of-the-word-rhubarb]

Thyme

Originally published as "Clearing" in the *Ocean State Review*, Fall 2010.

Raspberry

Originally published as "The Hunter: a ritual purging of Galway Kinnell's poem, 'The Bear' in *Spoon River Poetry Review*, edited by Kristen Hotelling Zona and Steve Halle, Spring 2018.

Dead Nettle

Published as "Homecoming: shadowing Muriel Rukeyser's 'Falling for Icarus,' in *Spoon River Poetry Review*, edited by Kirsten Hotelling Zona and Steve Halle, 2018.

Amaryllis

Originally titled "Future Anterior" with an epigraph by Julia Kristeva: "Although impossible and elitist, [the future anterior] is the only way for a speaking animal to shift the limits of its enclosure."

St. John's Wort

Published as "Dark Thinking Through Daylight," *Copper Nickel* (Issue 8), edited by Jake Adam York, 2007. Subsequently published as "Rumor" in *Black Clock, (no. 6)*, 2006 edited by Ariel Greenburg.

Rose

Originally published as "A glassful of tea and sugar in the mouth" in *The New Republic*, February 2016.

Dandelion

Originally published as "I Live in a Borrowed and Often Tender Multiplicity (sculpting Clark Coolidge)" in the *Boston Review*, selected by Tyrone Williams, March 2015. Subsequently appears in my book *Everywhere Here and in Brooklyn: A Four Quartets*, Belladonna Collaborative, 2012).

Rosemary

Published as "u n ( ) c o n s c i o u s" in the limited edition chapbook, Alter()Body, designed by Karen Randall's Propolis Press, 2010. Reference is to *Civilization and its Discontents* by Sigmund Freud, 1930. A soundscape of this poem was composed by Steven Brent and is included on the album, "Even the Failures are Beautiful"
[https://www.writing.upenn.edu/pennsound/x/Prevallet.php].

Frankincense

Published as "The Way of Screens" in *Songs of the Shattered World: The Broken Hymns of Hastur* edited by John Thomas Allen et al., 2016.

Aspen

Published in the limited edition chapbook, *The Black Dot*, designed by Jae Mae Barizo's Field Press, 2014.

Lobelia

Published as "Solstice Dream Solace"
[https://spacecraftproject.com/wp-content/uploads/2016/06/new-work-by-kristin-prevallet.pdf]

Pine

Published as "Logos Chakras" in *Salt* (#2), edited by Billie Chernicoff, 2021.

Sage

Published as "Flicker" in *The Doris* edited by Tamas Panitz and Billie Chernicoff, 2019. Inspired by bpNichol's conception of *Borderblur*: "Poetry which arises from the interface, from the point between things." He writes: "Of course the alphabet is a narrative—that movement thru your ABC. And any word you write is a displacement of that primary narrative." From "Narrative in Language" in *Meanwhile: The Critical Writings of bpNichol*, edited by Roy Miki, Talonbooks, 2002, p. 392.

About the Author

K (Kristin) Prevallet (born 1966) is a contemporary American writer living in Gloucester, MA. She is a scholar and practitioner of somatic arts who works across the mediums of language, performance, collage, video, soundscapes, and hospitality. K has published four collections of poetry, including *I, Afterlife: Essay in Mourning Time* and *Everywhere Here and in Brooklyn: A Four Quartets*; she is the archivist and editor of the complete ballads and songs of Helen Adam (*A Helen Adam Reader*); in addition, she has written two books which integrate poetics and the healing art of hypnosis: *Trance Poetics* and *Visualize Comfort: Healing and the Unconscious Mind*. To see more of her work, visit www.are.na/k-prevallet.

www.ingramcontent.com/pod-product-compliance
Lightning Source LLC
Chambersburg PA
CBHW060529080526
44586CB00012B/673